MINDING YOUR OWN BUSINESS

A Contemporary Guide to Small Business Success

MINDING YOUR OWN BUSINESS

A Contemporary Guide to Small Business Success

HERBERT S. MEYERS

DOW JONES-IRWIN
Homewood, Illinois 60430

ISBN 0-87094-563-7

Library of Congress Catalog Card No. 84-70599

Printed in the United States of America

1 2 3 4 5 6 7 8 9 0 ML 1 0 9 8 7 6 5 4

Preface

The purpose of this book is to increase the probability of your success in the task of owning and operating a small business. The book is directed both to the person who is now running such a business and to the person who is considering starting one in the future.

Our teaching experience in the field of entrepreneurship indicates that this book will be particularly helpful to readers who are willing to withhold, at least temporarily, their preconceived ideas about business, however formed. An incredible amount of literature on entrepreneurship has been published in recent years. Almost all of it has been dramatic, playing on the public's thirst for the romance of the classic rags-to-riches story. Moreover, much of the teaching on the subject has tended to generalize from highly individualized and incomplete histories. In reviewing this material, one must pause first to evaluate the validity of such glamorous but fragmentary documentation and then again to make the more personal judgment concerning the relevance of this information to a specific set of goals and objectives.

Further caution is warranted by another consideration. As we will point out, we are living in a world that is changing at an almost unbelievable rate. New technology has a daily impact on how we live, how we think, how we work. The present and projected economic and cultural environment of the United States differs in so many respects from the environment of earlier years that to rely on the old ways, merely because they served us well in the past, just doesn't make sense. Before reaching for the road map, one must be certain that the new highways are noted.

This book offers a fresh approach to the subject of small business management. It recognizes that many of the persons involved in small business differ from their predecessors in education, background, and even attitudes toward work. It acknowledges that today, more than ever before, the choice of a career in small business represents a deliberate decision rather than an unavoidable necessity. And above all, it responds to the fact that the new technology, the new affluence, the new lifestyles, and the new attitudes are reshaping, not only how we work and how we live as consumers, but indeed how we look at life. Together these factors demand a new way of reacting to the business challenge.

It is our contention that success in today's competitive environment requires awareness, creativity, intelligence, and a thoughtful appraisal of difficult and elusive information as well as the traditional hard work. What we ask of the reader is a willingness to consider the suggestions offered here objectively, the patience to familiarize himself with the requisite technical terms and procedures, and the commitment to use his mind to master what is presented. Because the dynamic character of the society in which we operate makes simple rules questionable, the balance of this book leans strongly toward a conceptual approach.

The book was originally designed as a text for a course at the New York University School of Continuing Education. Over the years, the students in this course have come from a great variety of backgrounds. They have included recent college students and persons about to retire after a lifetime in the corporate world—schoolteachers, computer analysts, entertainers, corporate executives, secretaries, and all things in between. While perhaps 3 to 4 percent of the students had not completed college, some 30 to 35 percent held advanced degrees in fields ranging from biology to art history. A significant number of MBAs enrolled in the course because the professional business school's orientation toward big business had left them with an unsatisfied appetite for information about the smaller, more appetizing alternative.

What held these students together was a common interest in the opportunities provided by small business. For the course and the book to work, for the approach presented to be valid, there must be great nontechnical similarities in the principles required to run a bookstore and an audio-video production company, a beauty salon and a computer brokerage firm, a restaurant and a research and information center, an art gallery and an employment agency, a boutique and a real estate office. For those who are willing to venture but have no specific venture in mind, there must be a way of identifying new small business opportunities that is generally applicable and yet is able to satisfy a wide variety of personal requirements. And for those who are already operating their own small businesses, there must be a way of thinking, benchmarks, and guidelines that can be utilized with equal validity in widely varying circumstances.

We feel that there is a way of looking at things that works for all small businesses, a method of going about the management task that crosses occupational boundaries. We feel that the head of a software company and the owner of a discotheque can discuss their common business problems, that a publisher can deal with the marketing challenges of an appliance repair service. We have seen such interchanges in operation and have found them exhilarating.

While the various ideas, approaches, and techniques presented here are applicable in all business situations, the primary thrust of this book is toward the small firm somewhere in what is now loosely regarded as the service industry. We make no direct reference to manufacturing processes because we see little reason to distinguish between the conduct of a service business and the conduct of a manufacturing concern in areas outside production. The difference between the marketing of goods and the marketing of services lies in the application of principles, not in the principles themselves. Our major departure from other works on business is that we carefully distinguish the small firm from the larger industrial enterprise that has heretofore served as the focal point for most serious works on business theory. In our efforts to include the most recent thinking on the subject, we have sought out those areas of contemporary business investigation, academic and practical, that have significant application to the smaller company, reinterpreting the relevant material in the light of the distinctive characteristics of the small business. We have reviewed the literature, observed the most brilliant theorists and practitioners, and then asked, "Will this work for a small business?" In this sense, this book is not innovative. We did not feel that it was necessary to reinvent the wheel but only to determine what kind of wheel would work for our particular conveyance.

Perhaps because of a personal bias, we avoid the use of the term *entrepreneur* throughout. In our view, this term, whose modern usage was introduced by Joseph Schumpeter several decades ago, now has unhealthy implications for the typical small businessperson because of its emphasis on rapid initial growth at the expense of sound management practices. Our focus is on the continuing business, and while strong growth must always be an integral part of such an enterprise, we favor the kind of growth that considers short-term profits as the opportunity capital of the future. While we have great admiration for the "take the money and run" spirit, we do not dwell on that limited business objective.

This book differs from many other works in its field in other important respects. With the exception of the discussions concerning the development of a business plan, it is not a conventional "how to" book. While it imparts a comprehensive understanding of the technical aspects of business, it does not do so with the presumptuous intention of bypassing the accountant or the lawyer. It does not deal with the rules for double-entry bookkeeping; it does not detail the procedures necessary to incorporate a business. It provides a workable grounding in profit and loss statements, balance sheets and cash flow, break-even, and ratio analysis; it discusses the various kinds of business entities (corporations, partnerships, etc.) and their respective legal and tax advantages; and it deals with such specific elements of the marketing mix as consumer research, advertising, and public relations. But such matters do not constitute the central thrust of the book.

As we have indicated, being in business is an interesting, absorbing, exciting, challenging, and potentially remunerative occupation. It embodies the drama of high-stakes poker and the demands and excitement of an intimate and fulfilling relationship, the thrill of meeting and overcoming the unexpected and the satisfaction of solving a complex puzzle. But because being in business is by its very nature an experience in dynamics, because it represents a foray into the constantly changing environment, what ongoing success in business requires is not the mastery of a series of static technical rules but a conceptual understanding of the essence of the business challenge that enables the astute manager to draw primarily on his own intelligence, experience, education, and creativity to move his enterprise forward. Frustrating though this may be to the person who comes to business education seeking a specific formula for success, it is our contention that a successful small business is not the result of well-learned technical skills but a personal expression of the mind, the force, the striving, and the creative ability of its managment.

We have therefore placed our major emphasis on the requirement for individual initiative as the means for the small businessman's success in today's competitive environment. How does *he** define *his* business so that *he* can compete effectively, continually? What strategies can *he* employ that will move *him* toward his objectives? How can *he* marshal *his* resources to achieve maximum strength? These and similar questions are the substance of the challenge to today's small business enterprise, and it is such questions that are primarily addressed by this book.

ACKNOWLEDGMENTS

I am deeply indebted to many people for their help in the creation of this book. While I cannot hope to mention all of them, I would like to mention the most important.

*We have used masculine pronouns throughout for efficiency. No male/female distinction exists in our approach to the subject.

Many teachers and writers have been involved in my education up to and including the Harvard Business School, and all of them have influenced the way I see things, the way I write. Specifically, however, I feel that it is impossible to write a book on contemporary business without reference to Peter F. Drucker, Theodore Levitt, and the late Abraham Maslow. While they should in no way be held responsible for my conclusions, their various marks should be in evidence. I find all of their works as fresh now as when they were first written.

My students at NYU and my associates at Meyers Manufacturing Company, particularly my brothers, Murray and Norman, have made many invaluable contributions to this effort—challenging my ideas and expanding my thinking. I look forward to a continuation of this interchange.

Andrew E. Norman, Craig Diamond, and Professors Cynthia and Martin Deutch have had a direct impact on this book, for which I thank them. Gladys Mills of Gotham Realty has continually offered a sense of practical business realism that has been helpful in all my endeavors. Carol Weinshel has nursed this manuscript from beginning to end with an efficiency and devotion that I sincerely appreciate.

And finally, my wife, Vivian, and my children, Sarah, Fred, and Andrew, have been their normal selves—supportive, stimulating, and, as always, perfect in all ways.

Herbert S. Meyers

Contents

1 Is owning a small business for you? The opportunity and the challenge

To help you determine whether a small business is for you, we will investigate three areas:

1. The current opportunities for small business.
2. The nature of the small business challenge.
3. The personal qualities relevant to success in small business.

THE CURRENT OPPORTUNITIES FOR SMALL BUSINESS

For the small businessman, the economic picture in the mid-80s is encouraging. We have emerged from what Schumpeter termed a period of "creative destructiveness"—a downturn in the business cycle in which the economy sheds its old skin and dons a new one.

The downturn of the early 80s

The pressures that created this downturn have abated. There is now a sense of optimism among the survivors of the recession, and optimism is also projected by the host of new entrants into the business community. As 1983 ended, a multitude of surveys indicated that both businessmen and economists, while unable to agree on the reasons for the recession, felt hopeful about the years immediately ahead. A Dun & Bradstreet study of 1,470 business leaders recorded the highest "Sales Optimism" index since the second quarter of 1979, and 15 leading economists interviewed by *The New York Times* expressed optimism regarding economic growth, interest rates, and employment figures.

We will not analyze all of the forces that contributed to the recent recession, but it is important to note why more businesses failed in 1981, 1982, and 1983 than at any time since the Great Depression. A significant number of those failures can be explained by traditional business cycle theory. When a country enjoys a boom period, such as the one that ended in mid-1981, economic momentum sustains a number of weak firms. Such firms, swept along by the generally strong business conditions, compound the inefficiencies of their operations when the economy is accelerating, yet are able to survive for a while. Eventually, however, they are felled by their own excesses. Loose business practices, characteristic of boom periods, no doubt helped to fuel the recent recession. The thinning of the business population during that recession provides both a lesson and an opportunity.

Unfortunately for some, fortunately for others, this simple explanation tells only a small part of the story. Without attempting a full explanation, it is important to point out that when Schumpeter referred to shedding the old skin and donning the new, his explanations for that process were considerably more fundamental than the "weak firm" explanation.

In order to understand the 80s, in order to appreciate the opportunities inherent in "creative destructiveness," it is important to consider three other elements of the socioeconomic scene, three other threads that work their way through our cultural fabric. We will discuss them together under the subject of change—technological change, demographic change, and attitudinal change. It is essential for the small businessman to consider these areas of change because within them lie the most significant opportunities for small business: it is easier and infinitely more rewarding to move with a trend than against one. While the thrust of inevitable change is a major factor in downturns of the business cycle, it is an equally important component of upturns. So change has two roles: it explains where we are in the economy, and it generates major opportunities for the future.

Technological developments

Changes in technology are perhaps the easiest to see. For our purposes in this chapter, two major implications of the current technological revolution must be considered.

As a society matures, it moves from a dependence on physical strengths to a dependence on intellectual abilities and repositions itself technologically. Concurrently, the level of affluence rises, and inexpensive labor loses its importance as a basic resource. The United States in the 80s has moved from a base in industrialism to a base in the service industries. Industrial man has given way to the postindustrial person.

This is now a fundamental part of our culture. Quite apart from the technological developments that spawned it, it has implications for all aspects of our society, from educational requirements to work habits. As the new technology has displaced the old, it has disrupted the lifestyles that originated in the old industrial base, supported its ethic, and responded to its demands on society. As the fires that fueled the smokestacks have been banked, a new way of living has emerged.

It is also obvious that the new technology has given rise to new opportunities. In *The Coming Boom*, Herman Kahn, the late director of research for the Hudson Institute, cited several areas that are now ripe for exploitation. He predicted major growth in:

1. Energy—derived from conventional and unconventional sources, including coal, geothermal sources, fusion, and fission.
2. Protection of the environment—ranging from sewage treatment to the reduction of pollution caused by industry and transportation.
3. Food and agriculture—ranging from new agricultural methods to the unconventional production of unconventional foods such as cheap proteins and edible plants that thrive in salt water, all the way to the biotechnologies.
4. Space—ranging from satellite activities and communications to the exploitation of low-temperature applications.
5. Medicine and health care.
6. Mass transportation.
7. Materials—fibers, foams, ceramics, molecular coatings, and so on.
8. Silicon chips.
9. Home, office, and factory automation and what Kahn refers to as the C^4I^2 Systems, the new generation of computers that will combine the command, control, communications, and computing functions with information and intelligence.

The revolution in modern business arising from new technology is so far-reaching that every business, no matter how small, will be dramatically different within the next 10 years. It is impossible to think about business, for example, without noting that there will be some

7.5 million personal computer–equipped homes by the end of this year, and that IBM estimates that the number will reach 22 to 24 million next year. Accepting the fact that yesterday's phenomenon, overnight mail delivery, is now giving way to electronic message carriers is only a beginning in realizing the dynamics of change.

Demographic changes

Demographic change is less spectacular but no less significant. Over time, changes take place in the demographics of a society; the balance of age within the population, geographic distribution, affluence, educational level, the makeup of the work force, the occupations and preoccupations of the people. Such changes demand a new allocation of resources. Many businesses suffered because of a failure to make the necessary adaptations in recent years; opportunity clearly exists for new and aggressive responses to demographic change.

Demographic change is continuous. Demographic developments, such as the rapid increase in the birthrate following World War II, have an unusually sharp impact on the rates of economic change; other demographic developments, such as the rising numbers of women in the work force, have a more gradual effect. Increases in marriages and divorces and in single and unmarried-couple households, the "graying" of the population, the geographic movement to the South and West, and the rising level of affluence all affect the nature, size, shape, and location of markets. Without studying these demographic changes, without acknowledging, for example, that by 1990 the households of the 35-to-44 age group will be the largest segment in the population with income in excess of $75,000 (831,000) or that there will be more than 1 million more households with income in excess of $75,000 in 1990 than there were in 1981, one cannot address the future of small business intelligently. In considering small business today, the overwhelming new reality is that the emerging fragmentation of society means that there are more differences between various groups of consumers than there are similarities. The mass market as we have known it is dying; it is being replaced by a host of new and individual markets that require new definitions, new approaches. (See Table 1–1 for data on some major U.S. demographic changes.)

Attitude shifts

The relatively new field of psychographics, the measurement of attitude, provides an approach to the understanding of this change in

TABLE 1-1 U.S. demographic changes*

Population change 1970–1981

Under 6	– 3.3%
6–17	– 12.9
18–24	+ 27.4
25–34	+ 56.8
35–49	+ 10.1
50 and over	+ 21.2

Geographical growth

	1979–1980	1980–1990 (projected)
New England	+ 4.2%	+ 7.3%
Middle Atlantic	– 1.1	– 7.7
East North Central	+ 3.5	– 0.4
West North Central	+ 5.2	+ 10.6
South Atlantic	+ 20.4	+ 9.6
East South Central	+ 14.5	+ 24.5
West South Central	+ 22.9	+ 25.3
Mountain	+ 37.1	+ 31.9
Pacific	+ 19.8	+ 16.4
United States	+ 11.4	+ 9.6

Traditional family (percentage of total households)

	1970	1981
Married-couple family	70.5%	59.8%
Male-headed family	1.9	2.3
Female-headed family	8.7	11
Nonfamily—male	6.4	11.3
Nonfamily—female	12.4	15.5
Numerical total	63,401,000	82,368,000

Income distribution (percentage of total households)

	1970	1980
$25,000 and over	4.6%	35.5%
$15,000–24,999	16.0	29.4
$10,000–14,999	26.6	14.7
Under $10,000	52.8	20.5

TABLE 1–1 ***(concluded)***

Employment and income by family type (1981)

	Employment	Percent change, 1979–1981	Median weekly earnings	Percent change, 1979–1981
Total families with earners	40,597,000	− 0.1%	$434	+15.1%
Married-couple families	33,191,000	− 1.4	474	+16.5
Married couple—husband only earner	11,535,000	− 6.7	374	+16.1
Married couple—wife only earner	2,116,000	+21.4	179	+18.5
Married couple—husband and wife earners	16,006,000	+ 0.9	591	+19.2
Female-headed families	5,765,000	+ 5.9	241	+15.3
Male-headed families	1,641,000	+ 7.3	382	+13.0

Selected median family income

	1979	Percent change, 1969–1979
United States	$19,908	+107.6%
Colorado	21,485	−124.9
Texas	19,372	−128.2
Alabama	16,602	+128.5
Iowa	20,243	+124.5
Illinois	22,007	+100.8
New Jersey	22,830	+100.1
New York	20,385	+ 92.0
Connecticut	23,038	+ 95.1
California	21,479	+100.1

*All data from *Sales and Marketing Management 1982 Survey of Buying Power* (New York: Bill Publications, 1982).

another significant area. With characteristic insight, sociologist Daniel Yankelovich observed typical attitude shifts (see Table 1–2).

The technological, demographic, and attitudinal changes that have been taking place are significant in terms of both business cycle theory and the practical concerns of small business. Strategies for pursuing the opportunities inherent in these changes will be discussed in the

TABLE 1–2 Attitude shifts in the United States

		Year	Percent
1.	Disapprove of a married woman earning money if she has a husband capable of supporting her	1938	75%
		1978	26
2.	Four or more children is the ideal number for a family to have	1945	49
		1980	16
	Two children is the ideal	1936	29
		1980	51
3.	For a woman to remain unmarried, she must be "sick," "neurotic," or "immoral"	1957	80
		1978	25
4.	Would vote for qualified woman nominee for president	1937	31
		1980	77
5.	Condemn premarital sex as morally wrong	1967	85
		1979	37
6.	Favor decision making abortion at up to three months of pregnancy legal	1973	52
		1980	60
7.	Agree that both sexes have the responsibility of caring for small children	1970	33
		1980	56
8.	Approve of husband and wife taking separate vacations	1971	34
		1980	51
9.	Agree that "hard work always pays off"	1969	58
		1976	43
10.	Agree that "work is at the center of my life"	1970	34
		1978	13
11.	Would go on working for pay even if they didn't have to		
	Men	1957	85
		1976	84
	Women	1957	58
		1976	77
12.	Increase in level of anxiety and worry among young Americans 21–39 years of age	1957	30
		1976	49
13.	Agree that "the people running the country don't care what happens to people like me"	1966	26
		1977	60
14.	Agree that they "can trust the government in Washington to do what's right"	1958	56
		1978	60
15.	Experience a "hungering for community"	1973	32
		1980	47
16.	Americans have a "sour grapes" outlook on life	1970	38
		1980	19
17.	Agree that it is morally acceptable to be single and have children	1979	75

TABLE 1–2 ***(concluded)***

		Year	Percent
18.	Agree that interracial marriages are not morally wrong	1977	75%
19.	Agree that it is not morally wrong for couples to live together even if they are not married	1978	52
20.	Agree that they would like to return to standards of the past relating to sexual mores, "spic and span" housekeeping, women staying home and only men working outside the home	1979	21

Source: Daniel Yankelovich, *New Rules: Searching for Self Fulfillment in a World Turned Upside Down.* (New York: Random House), 1981. Used with permission.

next chapter. Suffice it to say here that the small business venturer who seeks to move forward in the 80s must view his markets through new prisms.

THE NATURE OF THE SMALL BUSINESS CHALLENGE

We do not want to imply that running a small business at this particular time is an easy task—keeping up with change is not all that is necessary.

Starting a business (and staying in business) is difficult—especially for small firms. The pattern of failures by number of years in business has been relatively stable: almost 61 percent of all the businesses that fail are new businesses, and between 53 percent and 60 percent of all the businesses that fail do so within the first five years of operation (the third and fourth years being the period of greatest danger).

There are many reasons for such failures, and these reasons are usually subsumed under the vague catchall "poor management." Although the most frequently cited cause is the inability to anticipate cash requirements, a more appropriate explanation is lack of understanding of the nature and complexity of business.

The most common misconception that leads venturers astray is the belief that a product orientation is the key to business success; that is, if you devise a good product or a good service, you will have a good business. (This is the "entrepreneurial trap.") Unfortunately, a product orientation is insufficient for business success, except perhaps in the very short run. The product or service is only one element in an ongoing business enterprise—significant certainly, but only one element. It is, as we will discuss later, a means to an end. Being in business is the task of managing such resources as a product idea on a continuing basis, and it involves a wide number of technical and conceptual skills. A book like this one is possible because these technical and conceptual skills are universal in application—they apply to the newsletter publisher, the art gallery manager, the restaurant operator, and any other person who is running a business. Being in business is a process, a continuing process, and it is the application of a *variety* of skills that is crucial for success in that process.

A typical problem situation is illustrative. A man goes on vacation to Location X—beautiful, peaceful, and so forth. He can't find a four-star restaurant anywhere and therefore reasons that Location X would be a great place to start one. On the basis of that assumption, with no research or market analysis, he tries to do so and fails. No one in that beautiful spot is interested in four-star restaurants. The quality of the product in this case proves irrelevant. Only when the market has been located and quantified can a business go forward with reasonable prospects of success. Only then should the owner move all of his resources, including his product, toward his objective.

Being in business is not an opportunity to exercise the ego. It is an all-encompassing project that calls for a combination of physical and intellectual effort, research, creativity, and determined practical application. The challenge to the small businessman is to distinguish between the glamour of being in his own business and the reality of creating a viable, ongoing enterprise. The desire to create something special must be viewed through the realistic business requirements of that task: market analysis, strategy, funding, personnel management. These are not abstractions of business theory but essentials of proper management. Focusing on a particular aspect of a proposed venture may satisfy its short-run needs but will inevitably fall short of the longer-range requirements of being in business.

There is a small body of literature that deals with such questions as these: "Should you be in your own business?" "Do you want to be in business?" "Are you temperamentally suited to owning and operating your own business?" Matters of this kind are almost a mandatory opening section in most books about small business. Some books go so far as to provide a checklist of weighted boxes—if you score between x and y, the answer is yes; if you score between y and z, the answer is no. We avoid this approach.

Sometime in each day, month, or year, as we examine our lives, our personal situations, each of us asks, "Is there a better way?" If our degree of frustration with life is high, we may pursue the question further, asking ourselves what we really want and how we can get it. Some of us even follow the thought beyond that, asking what we have a right to expect, given our personal limitations. We have already used the word *success* several times. This word has no meaning unless it is judged against a specific set of personal values and goals. Unless we are willing to examine our values and to devise goals consistent with those values, we cannot realistically anticipate business success, only anxiety and frustration. Simplistic goals such as more money are not enough—goals of this kind are open-ended and thus can never be satisfied.

We cannot emphasize the need for personal evaluation too strongly. It gets very tough out there, and if we cannot relate the inevitable problems and setbacks of a small business to a clearly chosen and potentially satisfying goal, these knocks may be too much for us. Return on investment is a key financial guideline when it is applied to capital; when it is applied to personal outlays—outlays of effort, emotion, time—it becomes even more significant.

We are approaching a unique period in American business life. During the 18 years between 1946 and 1964, a record 76 million Americans were born. This generation is now at the age level from which middle managers are drawn. But the Bureau of Labor Statistics estimates that the number of management jobs in business and industry will increase by only 21 percent (from 8.8 million to 10.5 million) from 1980 to 1990. At the same time, the population in the 35-to-44 age group will rise from 25.4 million to 36.1 million, a 42 percent jump. No matter how you shake it up, no matter how the economy improves, upward movement in the business structure is going to be impeded. It's clogged in the middle.

The opportunities inherent in being in your own business are obvious. For some, they appear even more obvious when viewed against the alternative of life in a giant corporation. By choosing to own and operate your own business, you can hope to

1. Make more money for similar effort.
2. Get out of a box, see your ideas through to completion.
3. Be your own boss, set your own hours.
4. Develop and display talents outside your specialty.
5. Advance technology, society.
6. Realize your creative drive.

Some of these objectives can be accomplished in various other activities, but it is possible to achieve all of them in your own business.

On the other hand, the risks are there too. You may lose money. Paperwork has increased as a result of government regulations, and cyclical economic activity has become a way of life, so your income may be irregular. Getting off your present career track can cause you to lose your position in the career race. Accepting the responsibility for your own business ideas can diminish your leisure time, confront you with the psychological costs of failure, or distract you from the specialty that you truly love. Moreover, corporate life has been changing—the monetary rewards for talent have been increasing at an enormous rate in enlightened corporations, and as job change has lost its stigma, some of those who have felt that their careers were blocked in their previous positions have been able to construct a more enticing corporate life elsewhere.

THE PERSONAL QUALITIES RELEVANT TO SUCCESS IN SMALL BUSINESS

If there is one key difference between participating in corporate life and owning a small business, it lies in the fact that in your own business, particularly a small business, you and you alone are ultimately responsible. In your own business, depth analysis frequently takes a back seat to on-the-spot decision making. Even if you have conscientiously delegated a task, if that task is not being performed satisfactorily, you cannot stop at locating the failure—you must correct it. If your business loses direction, you and you alone are responsible for getting it back on course; if it runs short of money, you are the one who must find more. While no one is standing in line for your job, there is no backup either.

There are many who insist on labeling the qualities that will identify the successful individual businessman. Such terms as *leadership, endurance, enthusiasm, versatility, people oriented, decision maker, instinctive, aware, and self-confident* are frequently contrasted to the terms *studied, analytical, technical,* and the like—the implication being that the successful businessman is a ball of fire who can move armies by virtue of his wonderful "active" attributes. There is only limited historical support for this contention—such terms tell only part of the story.

If there is a single reliable clue to the probability of an individual's success in a small business, it lies in the marriage of the terms *personal responsibility* and *personal satisfaction.* Most people who succeed in a small business enterprise do so, not because they have an unrelenting drive for money, but because they have a positive view of themselves that calls for a substantial degree of achievement; it is the harnessing of this drive that can lead to satisfaction in small business. The need for a creative outlet, the need to manage, the need for power, a capacity for empathy, an imperative toward action, commitment to an idea, and the ability to exploit opportunities to get things done are all characteristics of the most successful entrepreneurs. But the things that bring these characteristics into effective harmony are the need to achieve, a positive self-image, and the drive to realize your potential—the requirement of living up to your own high expectations.

Among those who derive satisfaction from owning and operating a small business, the need for self-actualization, the drive for self-fulfillment, is never-ending. It renews itself time and again; it escalates; and thus it provides the fuel that enables them to go forward. It is the one essential requirement for small business ownership.

SUGGESTED READINGS

Fromm, Erich. *To Have or to Be.* New York: Harper & Row, 1976.

Kahn, Herman. *The Coming Boom.* New York: Simon & Schuster, 1982.

Maslow, Abraham H. *Motivation and Personality.* 2d ed. New York: Harper & Row, 1970.

Schumpeter, Joseph Alois. *History of Economic Analysis.* New York: Oxford University Press, 1954.

Yankelovich, Daniel. *New Rules: Searching for Self-Fulfillment in a World Turned Upside Down.* New York: Random House, 1981.

Periodicals that are helpful on a continuing basis include: *American Demographics,* P.O. Box 68, Ithaca, NY 14851. *Inc.*, Inc. Publishing Company, 38 Commercial Wharf, Boston, MA 02110.

A complete list of SBA publications is available from SBA, P.O. Box 15434, Fort Worth, TX 76119. The available reports cover everything from prototype business plans to analysis of specific industries.

Statistical Abstract of the United States (Washington, DC: U.S. Government Printing Office), published annually, provides a sampling of statistics compiled by all agencies and bureaus of the government. If the *Statistical Abstract* does not contain the information you need, it will indicate where that information may be found.

Survey of Buying Power is published annually in July by Sales and Marketing Management Magazine, a division of Bill Publications, 633 Third Avenue, New York, NY 10065. It contains demographic information and projections, from the national level to the county level, on population, household income, and a variety of similar subjects.

2 The business definition: How to get there from here

The difference between thinking about being in business and being in business is the difference between a vague idea and the translation of that idea into a concrete reality. While it is possible for the small businessman to achieve his objectives by following his natural instincts, a safer and potentially more productive approach is to develop a formal business plan that takes into consideration the best of contemporary business theory and the practical experience of successful venturers.

ADVANTAGES OF THE FORMAL BUSINESS PLAN

The structuring of a formal business plan involves the creation of a three-tiered model that begins with the establishment of a business "definition," continues with the formulation of a business "strategy," and concludes with the delineation of a business "program." Each step in this process requires a full investigation of the current thinking and information in the small business area. Because a formal business plan requires the articulation of a business philosophy, matches that philosophy with an operating scheme, and relates internal operations to the cultural and competitive environment, it offers the small businessman several very distinct advantages over the instinctive approach:

1. It forces him to think his project through with a significant degree of objectivity.

2. It facilitates the use of a wider perspective by providing a method of examining personal beliefs in the light of observable business realities.
3. It offers a rationale for discarding cumbersome, irrelevant, and misleading business dogmas and replacing them with constructive, workable guidelines.
4. It creates an imperative toward specific action.
5. It carries within it the seeds of business vitality and continuity.

The basic building block of the formal business plan is the business "definition," a statement of *what the business is by describing what the business does.* This is a "task-oriented" approach; that is, it relates the functions of the business to the work that must be accomplished. The underlying principle of this approach is that the major operating responsibility of the owner of a small business is to coordinate all resources toward a specific end. Such an integration of effort cannot take place unless that end is defined in meaningful terms.

THE BUSINESS DEFINITION BASED ON A CONSUMER NEED

The construction of a viable business definition starts with this fundamental thesis: *The work of a business enterprise is the conversion of an actual or potential consumer want into an active and effective demand.* That conversion is achieved by focusing on a particular need or want and developing it into a source of revenue. Although this may seem to place disproportionate emphasis on the marketing aspects of business, it is crucial to recognize that only the interaction of the company and the consumer can create income; all other elements of the business system can only create costs. Thus for a business definition to be valid, it must start with a consumer need. From this standpoint, the product or service is not the major preoccupation of the manager but only the means by which a consumer need can be satisfied. The task of the business is to foster the interaction between the consumer and his need and the company and its solution to that need.

A clear understanding of the term *need* is central to this approach. As used here, this term is multifaceted. First, a need must relate to something that is basic and ongoing—food, warmth, shelter, safety, belonging, mobility, communication, identity, esteem, aesthetic satisfaction, and the like. Thus enterprises are in business to satisfy needs. Each broad need forms a market category.

Second, a need must be viewed from the perspective of the lifestyle of an individual consumer or a category of consumers, the *who* of the market. The dimensions of a particular lifestyle involve an individual's identity in terms of activities (work, social events, shopping, etc.), interests (family, fashion, community, etc.), opinions (politics, culture, etc.), demographics (age, city, size, etc.), and socioeconomics (occupation, income, etc.). Thus an alert company will see the need for food in relation to the lifestyle of a working mother in one way and the need for food in relation to the lifestyle of an affluent suburban couple in a completely different way. The need for security may mean one thing to Betty Jones, an elderly widow, and something entirely different to Sarah Smith, a young manager in a major metropolitan area. Whatever the need is, it assumes a workable form only when it is applied to a specific consumer. Thus the communication needs of Dr. Rose, a surgeon, Barbara Frost, a sales manager, and Joel Levin, a real estate broker, may be separate and distinct, and the businesses designed to satisfy those needs may have no relation to one another.

Third, the component parts of a need must be understood in terms of its specific appeals and benefits. The need for food embodies many qualities—price, convenience, nutritional value, and so forth. Thus the need for food is viewed through the eyes of a specific consumer with a subset of requirements that are of particular importance to her. These requirements, like the lifestyles mentioned in the previous paragraph, are derived from the attitudes and values that the consumer adopts as he interprets the realities of his existence. Typically, where lifestyle attitudes revolve around such matters as "my life, my way," enhancement of physical self and psychological self, and new perspectives on work, leisure, money, and mobility, product or service appeals relate to further breakdowns of consumer preference—taste versus price, function versus fashion, quality versus convenience, etc.

Thus, as a starting point in the development of a formal business plan, we have a business definition that might be expressed in this way: "I am in business to satisfy the communication needs of pediatricians who work in suburban New Jersey towns and who consider speed important," or "I am in business to satisfy the information needs of real estate brokers who specialize in. . . and who consider convenience important."

And while the next chapter will carry this thought to a more practical level, it is easy to see at this point that relating the need to various market segments, lifestyles, and demographic and psychographic profiles provides a sense of direction for the venturer. When the statement of need is supplemented by who, where, when, and how, what, and why considerations, it becomes possible to talk about what a business does.

The concept of building a business around a basic need provides a prism through which a market can be investigated. Consider the area surrounding a new condominium in terms of safety and security. Who lives there? What are their needs? What values are important to them? What business can you construct to satisfy those needs?

Think about the need for esteem—self-esteem and the esteem of others. How have recent attitudinal changes arising from new levels of education and affluence affected the need for esteem? Choose a consumer group and examine it from this perspective.

Take a business segment and look at it through the magnifying glass of the need for knowledge, communication. Break it down into subsets.

Examine all of these needs and your solutions to them in terms of possible change. With the needs firmly in mind, how does your business react?

This approach is clearly superior to the conventional definition of the business. If the owner says, "I am in the real estate business," what then? What does this business definition tell him he must do Monday morning? Suppose, on the other hand, that the owner says, "I am in business to satisfy the luxury housing needs of single people between the ages of 25 and 34." Research will then quickly develop the information that he needs in order to go forward: How do I reach the market; what is it looking for; what does it consider important? The business task becomes apparent.

The small businessman who says, "I run a beauty salon," has a very limited idea of the possible scope of his enterprise. But if he says, "I am in the business of satisfying the need for physical self-enhancement among working women in the downtown Pittsburgh area who don't have much spare time," he has a business definition that can lead to a huge variety of innovative services.

This approach does not preclude starting with a product or service idea. But it changes the perspective through which that idea is viewed. It makes little difference whether a food merchant in Chicago starts with the idea of being in the food business or starts with the idea of satisfying a need that he perceives at a particular Chicago location, provided that the food business he develops is related to a potential or existing need that he has identified. That need could relate to any one of the broader needs we have already mentioned, but what is essential is that the business relate to a concrete need, that it not exist purely as a restaurant, as an abstraction. The tighter the fit between the business and the need, the better the chances of success.

While the approach to defining a business presented in this chapter has been advocated by earlier writers and teachers, the current availability of inexpensive computers allows it to take on an almost revolutionary quality for today's small businessman.

Consider the bookstore owner, sensitive to shifting moods among persons with a need for communication, entertainment, and so on, who has already added videocassettes to his stock. Using his computer, he classifies his entire inventory according to a breakdown of his customer "need" profile. He can do this broadly if he chooses, using whatever characteristics seem relevant to purchasing patterns—work, age, lifestyle, and so on; or more narrowly—escape literature (romance, espionage, detective, western, etc.), information (design, cooking, reference, etc.), and so on; or even more narrowly (Le Carré, Steinem, Garfield, etc.). The profile can be constructed simply by developing an arbitrary but meaningful coding system and then recording transactions by this system as they occur, putting the purchaser's name and address into the machine simultaneously.

It seems obvious that the benefits of such a procedure can be substantial. Purchasing decisions can be made more efficiently by recapturing pertinent information. Upon the arrival of specific books, appropriate mailing pieces can be developed and then addressed by machine to the proper consumers.

IMPLICATIONS OF THE NEED-BASED BUSINESS DEFINITION

In developing this basic idea of a business existing to satisfy a need, we have departed from the conventional ways of looking at a business in three significant respects.

1. We have shifted the management emphasis from such useless titles as restaurant, boutique, audio-video production, publishing, and real estate and such service or product ideas as telephones, software, and brokerage to the challenging and creative area of business dynamics. We have taken the business out of isolation. The owner who says he is in the restaurant business or the ready-to-wear boutique business is uttering, in effect, a meaningless abstraction that serves only to give him a statistical identity on the occupation scale; such a statement provides no hint of what he must do to make his business successful. The owner who views his business in this way has no means for bringing focus to the complexity of the continuing business enterprise, for integrating the various business functions. His efforts are not guided by the basic fact that how you see the business, how you develop the total enterprise, is more important than the product or service. By concentrating on the satisfaction of a need, we establish a business purpose, a goal toward whose achievement the owner marshals his resources.

2. We have changed the way in which "profits" are regarded. Typically, most owners state that profits are the objective of a business, that "making money" is the reason for being in business. Thinking

along these lines develops a preoccupation with a subject that can do nothing to move the business forward. Furthermore, the goal of profits is too abstract to lead to any degree of satisfaction.

Profit, the satisfactory return on the owner's investment, is a *cost* of being in business in the same way as heat or electricity. It provides motivation for the owner, and it develops an asset that is needed for both growth and continuity.

But profit cannot be made if the company is not successful in its fundamental work. Unless a consumer need is satisfied, unless a demand is effectively converted into a source of revenue, the company cannot exist, much less prosper. Profit thus becomes, not the goal of the enterprise, but a test of the validity of the business plan.

As we have indicated, the product or service is offered as a means of satisfying a simple need or a combination of needs in a particular way. The marketer uses his best judgment to tailor this package of value satisfactions, including those costed aspects of function, convenience, service, and so on that he feels are necessary to make the offering desirable. He is, in effect, attempting to buy customers through his allocation of resources. If the resultant total service, including profit as a cost component, must command a price greater than the customer is willing to pay, then the marketer's assumptions concerning the consumer's behavior are incorrect—the idea is not valid, and the fit between the service and the need, the solution and the problem, must be reexamined. In seeking an explanation for a poor profit picture, the businessman questions his assumptions and the efficiency of their execution. Relegating profit to its proper role in the costing structure allows the business to concentrate on its chosen task.

3. By incorporating the concept of ongoing needs into our description of what the business does, we have avoided the costly trap of wedding the venture to a particular time or place. By viewing the product or service as a means to an end, a response to a need, we have built into the business definition a continuing requirement to reevaluate both the nature of the need and the means for satisfying it. When, in Levitt's classic illustration, the railroaders were locked into their narrow service definition, the idea that they were running railroads, they failed to respond to either the changing technology or the new manifestations of the need for mobility. Had they seen their business in broader terms, as meeting the need for mobility, their story might have taken a different turn.

Realistically, from the moment a product or service is conceived, it is on the way to becoming obsolete. Someone else is always out there who can follow your path cheaper and maybe better. Life changes, demand shifts, and the entrepreneur in love with a simple product idea is left with a personal romance. When we start with a need that is by definition timeless, even if a particular response to that need eventually gives way to another, the need itself continues to exist, and the alert business will adapt and persist.

SUGGESTED READINGS

Drucker, Peter F. *Management*. New York: Harper & Row, 1974.

_______. *Management for Results*. New York: Harper & Row, 1964.

Levitt, Theodore. *The Marketing Imagination*. New York: Free Press, 1983.

Loudon, David L., and Albert J. Della Bitta. *Consumer Behavior: Concepts and Applications*. New York: McGraw-Hill, 1979.

3 Strategy and creativity

A business strategy provides the framework for accomplishing the task implied in the business definition. It intertwines the two major lines of business activity by (*a*) setting out the avenue of approach to the targeted consumer and (*b*) relating that approach to the competitive environment.

Once we have located the need that we wish to satisfy, our next step is to devise a way of meeting the need that will give us an edge over similarly inclined competitors. As we pointed out in Chapter 2, even if a firm has the advantage of being the first to recognize a potential need, its business definition and its resultant strategy must incorporate the seeds of growth and flexibility that will enable it to deal with the future. It is prudent to acknowledge the fact that in a short time, competitors will enter the field or the nature of demand will shift—probably both. The planning sequence looks like this:

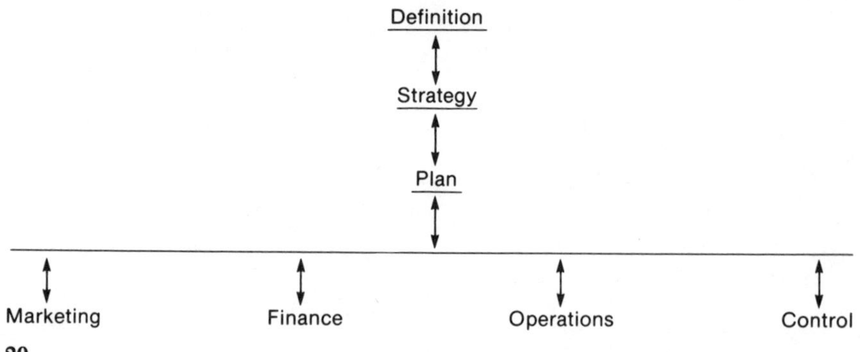

It is important to note that the arrows point in both directions. Review and reevaluation must be a part of the philosophical base of the firm's program, and the feedback from operations is a central element of such review.

Michael Porter describes the playing field on which this game plan must be executed in this way:

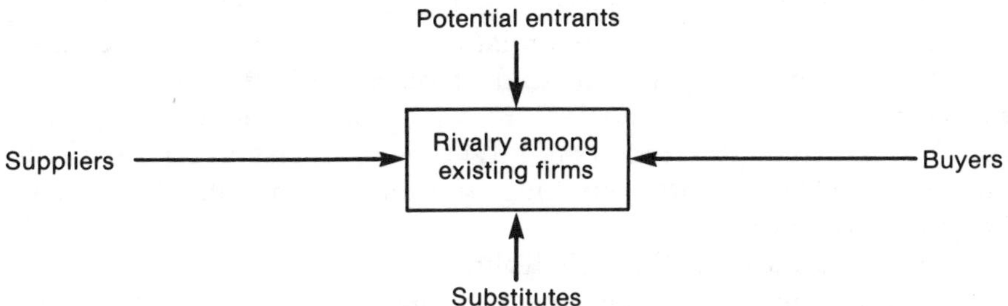

Source: Michael Porter, *Competitive Strategy* (New York: Free Press, MacMillan Publishing Company), 1980.

Each firm exists in a space alongside other firms bound by a similar business definition but offering varying strengths (strategies) in their efforts to reach the objective. At any one time, that space may be threatened by the entry of additional similar firms or by firms offering substitutes for the existing services. The quality of any particular firm's space is defined by the degree of its strength (effective strategy) vis-à-vis its rivals, suppliers, and buyers. The work of the manager is to develop his operation in the way that will put it in the most favorable position relative to these threatening forces. The success of the operation in reaching its goal, in fulfilling its definition, depends on how well the manager and his work force perform this function.

For a small business, the scope of the challenge defined by this model becomes immediately clear. When we examine the gamut of possible competitive weapons, it is obvious that in today's economic climate, the arsenal of the small business is extremely limited. It is in the search for a realistic approach to the problem of competition that the differences between small and big business are most apparent.

THE FOUR BASIC BUSINESS STRATEGIES

Generally speaking, there are four basic strategies: (1) legal and technological protection, (2) advantages of size, (3) differentiation, and (4) focus. These strategies are not mutually exclusive, and the use of more than one would be advantageous.

Legal protection in the form of patents or licensing restrictions would seem to be a relatively good course and should be pursued whenever possible. There are, however, major limitations to this strategy.

As a result of trends in government policy, the use of regulations, licensing, zoning permits, and the like as a means for limiting new entrants into a particular area appears to be losing force. Restrictions on establishments serving liquor or providing entertainment still exist in some major metropolitan areas, but the increased mobility of the population serves as an antidote to this form of protection.

At the current rate of technological innovation, patent protection works primarily when it is accompanied by a need for heavy capital investment. Moreover, the time and financial limitations of the small business place it at a decided disadvantage in the pursuit of patent protection. Although it may take little time or money to obtain a patent, if the patent is worth anything, substantial amounts of both will be required to defend it.

Effective protection through technology is also limited without a major capital investment, and the edge that was once to be gained by either unique experience or the requirements of high learning curves seems to have been dissipated by modern information systems.

Size is the key to many competitive strategies that are by definition not open to the small business. Primary among these are the cost advantages that come from economies of scale and the market dominance that can occur from the short-term shifting of resources or from economies of horizontal or vertical integration. The small businessman must accept the fact that price competition is not a viable strategy for him *except in the very short run*. While price competition may seem effective against larger competitors with different cost structures—the small discount retailer, for example, against the conventional department store—there is no basis for such an advantage against the competitor of similar size and inclination. Even those manufacturing companies that move to locations with more favorable labor rates can count on only a very short-range advantage.

Thus, by the process of elimination, product or service differentiation and focus become the two significant areas of strategic opportunity for the small business. (They are, in effect, two sides of the same coin, because focus is really a differentiation of the offering tailored to a need so particular that the defined market is not large enough to attract effective competition.) Both are viable strategic weapons because their effectiveness is derived from the key strengths of small business: creativity and flexibility.

The ease with which the strategy of differentiation can be utilized by the small businessman is directly related to the need-oriented definition outlined in the previous chapter. Market segmentation, the understanding of needs and of how they can be broken down into component parts, provides the key.

HOW CREATIVITY WORKS

Before dealing directly with the technique of formulating strategy, it is important to look at creativity, the requisite resource, to understand how it works. (How creativity is encouraged in an organization will be dealt with in Chapter 9.)

If we look at several of the marketing phenomena of recent years—the Pet Rock, the Slinky, the Hula-Hoop, the Frisbee, Eastern Onion, Rent a Wreck, the Erotic Baker, or Celestial Seasonings—a common thread seems to run through them. These products illustrate unusual situations, but they are relevant to our subject because each of them resulted from a new way of seeing a product or a market. (The Slinky, after all, was only engineering wire.) And while the ability to see existing things in a new way did not alone bring about success—each of these enterprises involved a trial and error process that demanded enormous mental and physical energy—the capacity to approach a market with a fresh, uncensoring mind was an aspect of all these endeavors.

The mental processes required for this task of innovative thinking are described by several different but closely related labels—creativity, intuition, imagination—but the predominant theories linking them together seem to have a common starting point: The conscious mind is a pattern-making system. It receives impressions from the environment, recognizes those impressions, and sorts them into patterns. Pour hot water over a square of Jell-O or wax. As you do so, patterns form on the surface. Subsequent pourings of hot water add to the patterns but do not change their basic structure.

Patterns are formed in the mind as information is received. Additional information is adapted to the existing patterns, building on what is already known. This is the system of logical development. Conventional education tells us that everything proceeds from the basic pattern. While the "right answers" that our educational system has taught us to grasp follow from the systematic accumulation of experience, it is obvious that their reference point can only be previously classified information, a traditional way of looking at things.

What we refer to as creative thinking starts with the ability—and the willingness!—to look at things, to examine the information our experience has accumulated, in a different way, either by breaking up the existing patterns or by looking at those patterns from another angle. *The creative person develops new patterns from accumulated information.* We all have the power to employ this creative capacity, but our mental inhibitions determine the degree to which we are able to do so.

BLOCKS TO CREATIVITY

There are blocks that limit our ability to see things in a fresh way, that inhibit us from absorbing new information, and in order to remove these blocks from our path, it is helpful to understand what they are.

A. *We tend to focus on one way of looking at a subject, to lock a particular picture in our mind with one conceptual view of recognition. And yet, when we examine that view, we note that it is very limiting. Think of an object, a figure.*

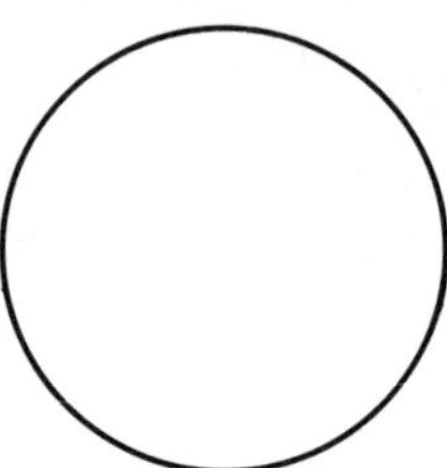

How many things can you see?

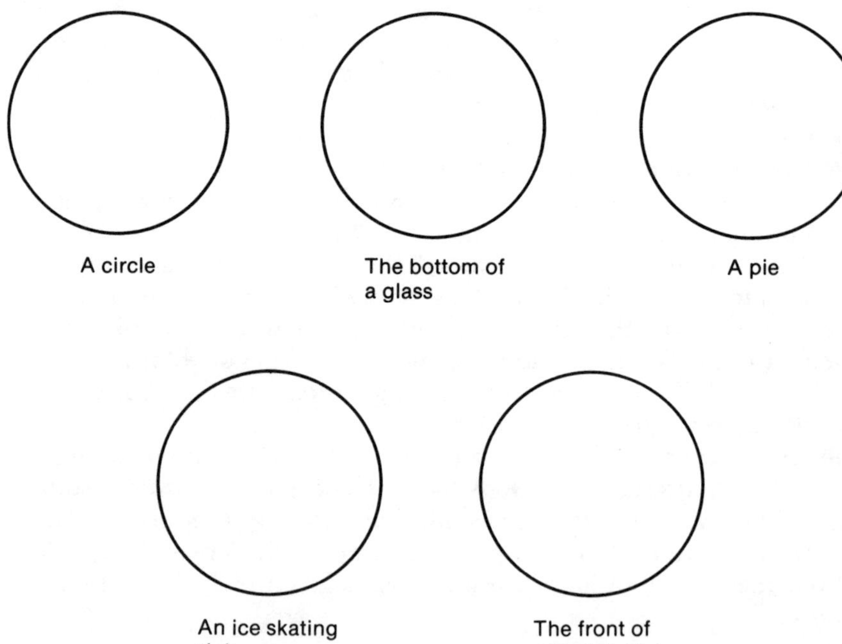

Or think of this figure.

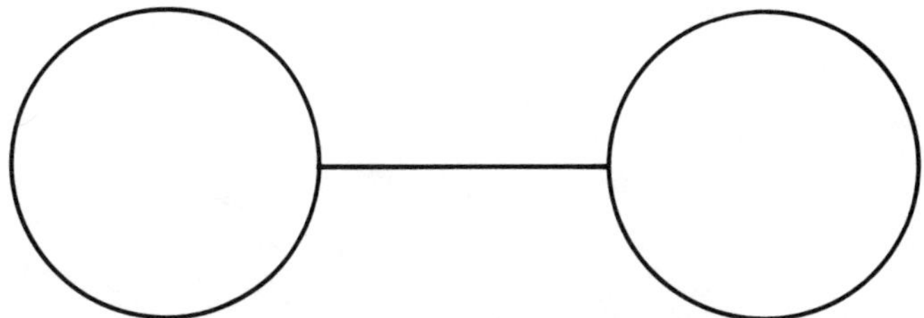

Source: Edward de Bono, *Lateral Thinking: Creativity Step by Step*. Copyright © 1970 by Edward de Bono. Reprinted by permission of Harper & Row Publishers, Inc.

1. Two circles joined by a line.
2. A line with two circles.
3. Two circles each with a short tail touching.
4. Two circles with long tails overlapping.
5. Two holes and a crack.
6. Two coins on a match.

B. Logical experience leads us to operate with certain assumptions that in fact may not apply in a particular situation.

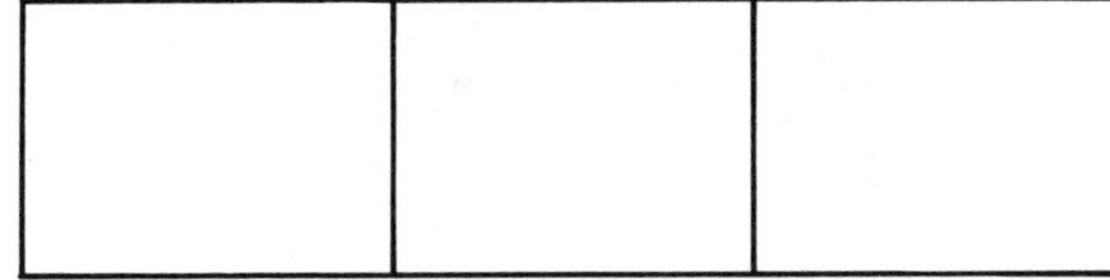

Using only these nine equal line segments, form three squares.

What stops most people from solving this problem is the assumption that the squares must be separate, although the directions say nothing to forbid overlapping.

Connect the dots with four straight lines without removing your pencil from the paper.

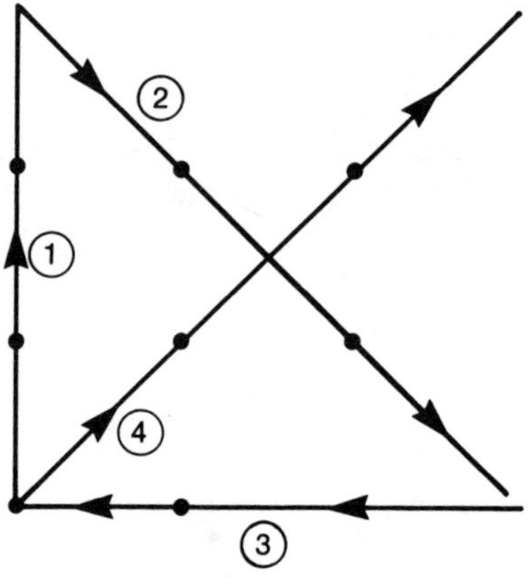

Source (for both of the above figures): Edward de Bono, *Lateral Thinking: Creativity Step by Step*. Copyright © 1970 by Edward de Bono. Reprinted by permission of Harper & Row Publishers, Inc.

This assumption that inhibits a solution here is that you cannot go outside the square implied by the positions of the dots.

C. We are likely to be overwhelmed by the entire picture when new solutions can be easily found by breaking the picture into parts. We see things as they are presented, as though they were inviolable, when in fact they may serve our purposes better if they are broken down, restructured.

Divide this figure into four equal parts:

This problem is solved by breaking the figure down:

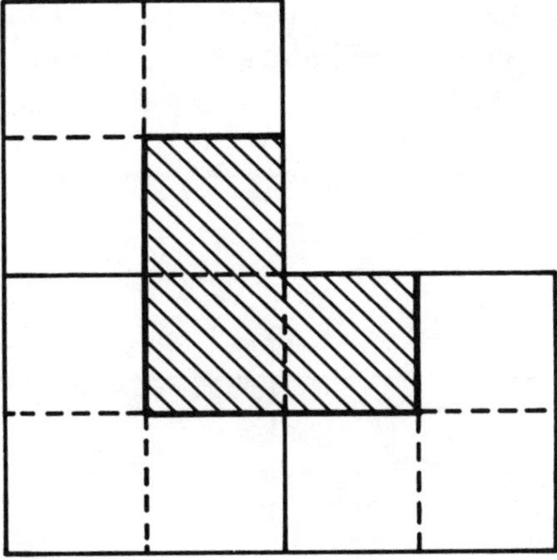

Source (for both of the above figures): Edward de Bono, *Lateral Thinking: Creativity Step by Step*. Copyright © 1970 by Edward de Bono. Reprinted by permission of Harper & Row Publishers, Inc.

Form these existing objects into a single easy-to-describe shape.

The limiting assumption here was that the shapes had to be handled exactly as they appeared, that they could not be broken down. Frequently the problem cannot be solved by merely rearranging elements. The parts must be examined individually and restructured into a new whole.

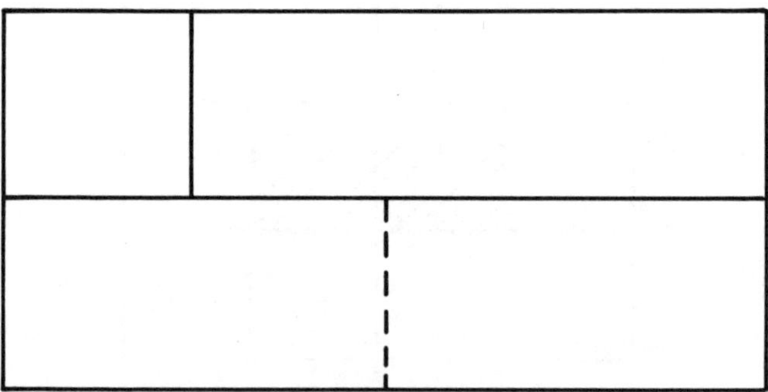

Source (for both of the above figures): Edward de Bono, *Lateral Thinking: Creativity Step by Step*. Copyright © 1970 by Edward de Bono. Reprinted by permission of Harper & Row Publishers, Inc.

D. We tend to stop when we have an answer without proceeding to the question of whether it is the best answer. Yet the first solution is not necessarily the best solution. If we are attempting to divide a square into four equal parts, for example, there are many solutions. Here are some, devise others:

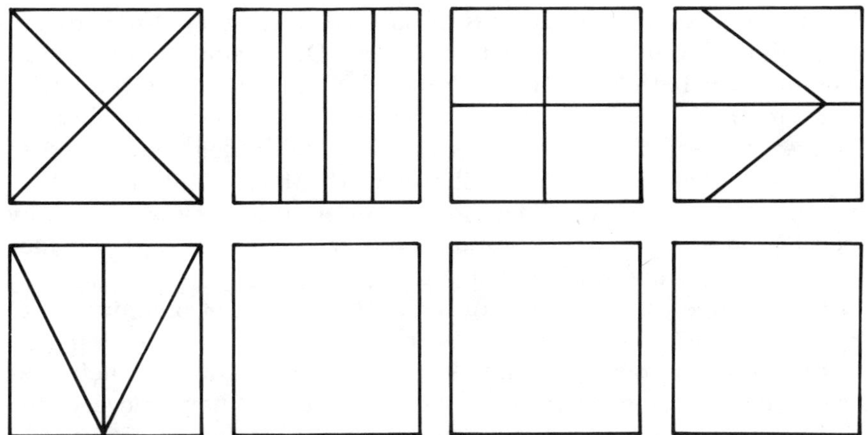

Source: Edward de Bono, *Lateral Thinking: Creativity Step by Step*. Copyright © 1970 by Edward de Bono. Reprinted by permission of Harper & Row Publishers, Inc.

Almost the only constant requirement here is that at least one line must go through the center of the square. Think of other solutions.

THE APPROACH NEEDED FOR CREATIVITY

For creativity to take place, it is necessary to focus on the problem as though it had never been attacked before. Because no one has done just this, or because no one has done it this way, does not mean that it can't be done. Times change, markets change, capabilities change. If a person is seeking a better way, it is absolutely essential that he not allow his mind (or his audience) to impose negativism on his thinking, particularly in the early phases. This is sometimes referred to as judgment deferral. Creative thinking differs from our normal process of logical thinking in that it welcomes incorrect or wild, impractical ideas because consideration of such ideas frequently leads to approaches that become workable solutions. Where logical thinking depends on step-by-step analysis, with each new move stemming from a "right" or provable point, creative thinking seeks new points of departure.

Problem: An elimination tennis tournament has 111 entries. The organizer confronted with time and space problems has to determine how many matches will take place. A first round of 55 with one player drawing a bye will produce 56 eligible for a second round of 28 matches, followed by a third round of 14 and a fourth of 7. Then what? How about a first round of 32 matches, with 23 byes? The mind reels. But if one remembers that every player except the winner is going to lose, and lose just once, it immediately becomes obvious that there will be 110 matches, however they are structured—and this knowledge will make it easy to design the format.

This same kind of thinking is often used in mystery stories to uncover the solution. In the Arthur Conan Doyle story *Silver Blaze*, everyone was baffled by the midnight theft of a valuable racehorse; none of the people around the stable heard a sound. For Sherlock Holmes, the significant fact was that the stable dog did not bark, which suggested that it was familiar with the thief. Similarly, in dealing with a marketing problem, you can often find a new approach by focusing on an individual consumer, one who does not bark for your competitor's products. How can you move him?

The creative person understands that the purpose of planning is not to be right but to be effective. The distinction is important. Being effective must, of course, eventually involve being right, but being effective means being right only at the end rather than at every step along the way. The need to be right all the time is the biggest impediment to the development of new ideas.

To force the mind to work creatively, as we have pointed out, requires the imposition of a temporary censorship on our natural inclination (*a*) to see things as we have always seen them and (*b*) to limit our thinking to step-by-step logic. We can move in this direction by asking ourselves a series of questions as we seek new awareness, questions that are intended to force answers to the basic question "How else can I look at this?" Because it is sometimes difficult to achieve this breakdown of normal patterns, devices such as those outlined by Milton Fisher in his book *Intuition* are encouraged. Fisher's methods include exercises leading to deep relaxation and dream recall, but they also include such simple devices as the repetition of the word *why* in the course of the thinking process.

The constant call to action is inherent in the business process, and nothing tends to perpetuate old myths, old directions, more than this incessant demand for movement. Taking time to think, to seek new approaches, is all too often sacrificed because of immediate but less important demands. In their excellent book *The Art of Japanese Management*, Richard Pascale and Anthony Athos dwell extensively on this point: "The Japanese image of a good decision maker is the man who can resist the drive for closure until he really sees what's required." An important business skill in their analysis is "indefinition." (More material on the subject of indefinition may be found in various works on Zen and Taoism.)

METHODS FOR APPLYING CREATIVITY TO BUSINESS STRATEGY

Now, let's move to the practical application of intellectual creativity to the problem of strategy in the competitive environment of the small business, dealing particularly with the requirements for differentiation and focus.

Reverting to the need-oriented approach outlined in Chapter 2, it is most productive to consider an industry as an assemblage of firms that have developed a group of responses to a basic need. We then begin our investigation with an industry based on a food need, a health need, a safety need, and so on.

In attempting to develop a strategy that will be effective within that assemblage, we may employ any or all of four different methods of viewing the industry.

1. Examine the ongoing areas of central importance—the breakdown of the industry into its key components—seeking a weakness or a point of vulnerability.
2. Examine the industry from different points of view, seeking a new entry point.
3. Examine the way the industry operates, seeking a breakthrough in terms of assumptions.
4. Examine the dynamics of the industry, seeking an opportunity through the uncovering of a new answer.

I. Examination of the ongoing areas of central importance, the search for the key components, is the most basic method. It allows for a strategy in which the businessman marshals his resources on one or a very limited number of significant areas where concentration (at some expense to other areas) will give him an edge. This is the essence of differentiation.

The basic technique employed in this strategy is an offshoot of segmentation analysis. Using demographics, socioeconomic factors, lifestyle breakdowns, attitudes, product appeals, and psychographics, the industry is broken down by age, income, geography, lifestyle, or attitude, depending on the nature of the need. The need is then examined through the eyes of the various consumers, and the venturer selects his target need.

An excellent illustration of the technique may be found in a study prepared for Du Pont by the well-known analyst Maggie Fine. In this report, Fine separated dress consumers by their attitudes toward clothes. After interviewing more than 1,000 women, she differentiated seven attitudes and quantified them:

a. Clothes "Junkies" (11 percent)—use clothes to relate to other people; characterized by a need to be noticed, to be first, to dress "better"; shop often; respond to bargains, new fashion information.

b. Sophisticated Clothes Lovers (14 percent)—are confident about who they are; reflect a sense of style that is important to them; choose clothes that reflect self; derive pleasure from experimenting, being watched and admired.

c. Closet Clothes "Junkies" (15 percent)—differ from *a* (above) because of social and economic restraints; live through clothes but are afraid to take risks.

d. Defensive Dressers (14 percent)—are conscious of fashion but use clothes to take on the protective coloring of the environment, to blend in; have little taste of their own; are very insecure, unwilling to stand out; use clothes to guarantee proper classification.

e. Classic Individualists (15 percent)—have a functional, practical view of clothes, not emotional, not impulsive; see clothes as expressions of self-confidence; are likely to feel that they do not respond to fashion trends.

f. Troubled Users (15 percent)—have a self-defined figure problem, unresolved anxiety about their clothes, the way they look; are totally preoccupied with personal problems.

g. Couldn't Care Less (13 percent)—are inner directed, quite secure; dress functionally, unemotionally; are really not interested in clothes.

If demographic factors—age, location, income level—are imposed on such an attitude study, a variety of strategic approaches becomes obvious. You can try to choose an underdeveloped market segment; or you can try to choose the segment that best suits your particular personal and business strengths, your skills and resources; or you can make a winners-losers analysis: Which aspects of the industry are currently producing success?

There are a great many ways to effect such a dissection. What, for example, are the key benefits in automobile purchasing according to the customer?

Performance
Durability
Running costs
Comfort
Resale

Payment terms
Parts availability
Convenient sales
Convenient service. . .

Looking at it another way, what are the appeal segments of analysis by which you could look at a competitor?

Design
Price level
Marketing technique
Location
Service
Sales force
Production techniques
Financing
Image
Customer relationships

Within the guidelines of the differentiation strategy, once the market has been broken down as completely and imaginatively as possible, the aggressive small businessperson develops an edge by massing his resources on a particular segment—perhaps he abandons other elements to allow for this emphasis. He might, for example, give up manufacturing, buy the product, and concentrate on marketing. He might share distribution facilities and concentrate on design. He might concentrate on delivery, availability, or service.

II. Examination of the industry from different points of view involves the principle of nondirect confrontation. Here the method is to examine the major thrust of the competition and see whether there is another way in. If, for example, a product is involved, could a strategy of entry through service be successful? If the competitors' thrust is variety, could specialization be effective? Remember, we are talking about an entry point.

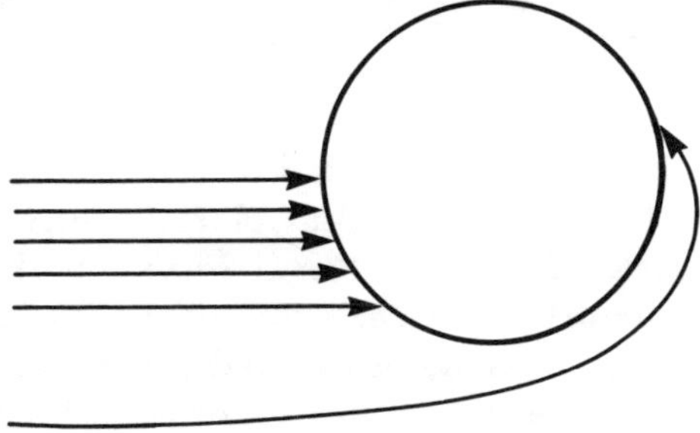

An interesting way of attacking this problem is illustrated in an approach outlined by Phillip Meyer, former director of news and circulation research for the Knight-Ridder newspapers. In attempting to segment the newspaper readers in a specified market area by psychographic factors, a study was undertaken to match the readers of existing newspapers to certain attitudes—in this case, attitudes toward modernism and traditionalism. Using such statements as "There are situations where sex outside marriage can be a healthy thing" and "I like to think I'm a bit of a swinger" to reflect modernism and such statements as "I often wish for the good old days when life was simpler" and "Young people have too much freedom today" to represent traditionalism, a profile of existing newspaper readership was developed. The attitudes shared by those people *who did not read* the existing newspapers defined a major area of opportunity for a new one: the dog that did not bark was discovered. The need for information was there, but among a certain psychographically identifiable group of consumers, it was not being met.

Think about other approaches to existing needs, about balloon bouquets and chocolate greeting cards instead of flowers. Is the gourmet takeout store another way of being in the restaurant business, of satisfying a certain target group's need for food?

III. Examining the assumptions of the industry involves upsetting the apple cart. Are there certain assumptions about how the industry does business that can be questioned? Here the tool can be an in-depth investigation of how the competitors operate internally or how they approach the need.

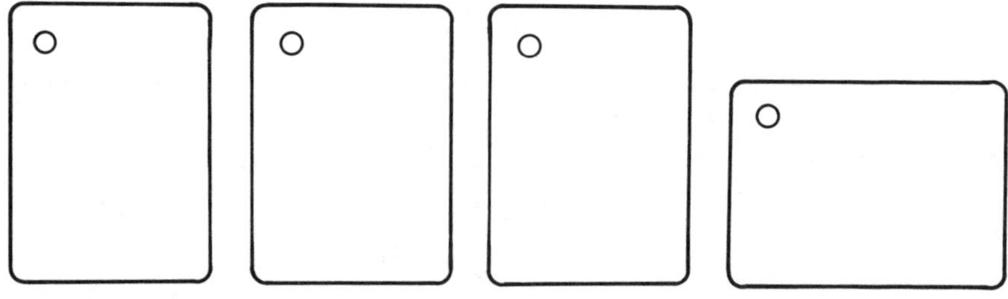

An instructive illustration is provided by the development of a company called Air Letter. Jim Hanifin, a Colorado entrepreneur, studied the sorting procedures of the U.S. Postal Service with a view toward improving his own courier service. Coming upon a weakness in the handling of long-distance mail, he evolved a new technique through which he could guarantee second-day delivery at a cost of $1.20 per letter by using a combination of Western Airlines and conventional local postal service. Through careful analysis, he found a new way to do something. (Unfortunately, this isn't always enough. With a service priced far below the competition, he launched his venture—only to discover that he had a crippling credibility problem. Few people believed that he could do what he promised to do for only $1.20. He hired a Los Angeles research firm, which discovered that 10 times as many people were likely to try the service at $4.25.)

A startlingly simple illustration dates back 100 years. Bridge building had made advances from the mid-17th to the mid-18th century as metallurgical technology evolved stronger and lighter materials and designs. But every material was soon extended to its limit, the length of span at which it could carry no more weight without additional bracing but at which the extra bracing began to outweigh the strength it added. No matter how strong and light the materials, there is a length limit beyond which the middle of a bridge will sag and the bridge will break. A century ago that limit was considerably less than the distance between Manhattan and Brooklyn. Roebling and others won the battle for longer bridges, not by fighting sag, but by giving in to it completely. Whereas the pressure on a rigid span is concentrated at the midpoint, the tension on a hanging steel cable is distributed along its entire length. Moreover, the tensile strength of steel (resistance to stretching) is far greater than its rigidity (resistance to bending). The invention of the suspension bridge stems directly from asking "Why does the roadway have to *be* the bridge? Why can't it *hang from* the bridge?" As an indication of how hard old thinking dies, we still say we "drove over the Golden Gate Bridge." We never did. We drove under it.

Why? Why? Why? Why does everybody do something a certain way? Why, for example, does the top row of keys on every typewriter consist of the ridiculous sequence *QWERTYUIOP?* When Christopher Latham Sholes was perfecting his invention in the 1860s, he found that fast typing caused certain letters to stick together frequently. Placing the *I* and the *O* next to each other and toward the end of the row slowed down the typist's striking of these very common and often sequential letters by some 20 percent and thus reduced the incidence of jamming. The mechanism with the sticking problem is now almost a collector's item, but its crazy keyboard is still standard, even on computers with no moving parts, because so many people were trained on it. Might some manufacturer or marketer offer the millions who do not know how to touch-type a modern instrument with a far superior keyboard? Maybe one with four rows of letters instead of three? Maybe one with a few high-frequency combinations, such as *IO* and *TH* or even *THE* and *TION*, on single keys?

Why were flashbulbs necessary? Do the original reasons still apply?

Did the Chinese restaurant industry develop because so few other places were open Sunday nights?

Why do European television sets produce sharper, clearer images than American sets? TV broadcasting burst into massive popularity in the United States in the late 1940s, and millions of sets were made and sold when technology could handle only a certain number of lines per inch of screen. Technology quickly advanced, and European TV, starting later, could and did use more lines per inch, with far better image resolution. The American industry, however, was trapped by the huge existing inventory of low-definition transmitters and receivers. Is it stuck there forever? If it could now produce sets with exactly twice as many lines per inch, might there be a market for sets that would reproduce standard broadcasts and tapes at least as clearly as standard sets but could also show tapes made on special equipment, computer readouts, and other materials with vastly increased clarity and sharpness? And if such sets sold in quantity, wouldn't TV stations find a way to transmit a signal compatible with both the old and the new?

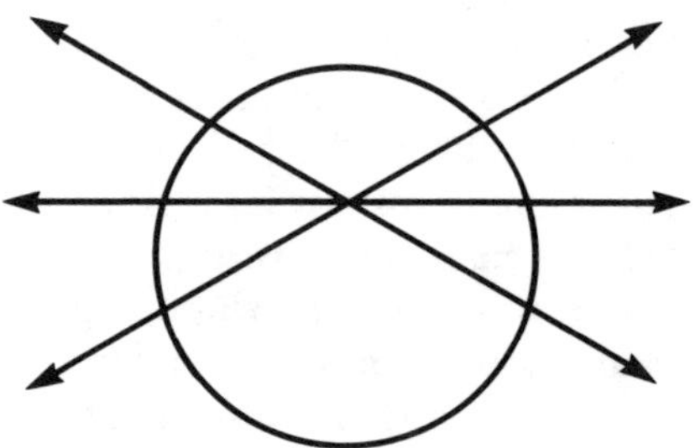

IV. The fourth method, examining the dynamics of the industry, treats the present industry approach as merely a first answer, not a final one. The proposed course is to go further, to keep on looking. The opportunistic businessperson seeks a competitive avenue by extending the market in a new direction, inspired by an observable trend in need, or style, or technology (demographic changes, changes in consumer tastes or energy costs, new materials). George Eastman did not invent celluloid, but he was the first to see that it could replace glass plates in photography and transform an expensive, cumbersome craft into an inexpensive, handy, and immensely popular pursuit. Eastman's first answer to the marketing of Kodak cameras was to sell them loaded for 100 exposures, after which the consumer would return the camera to the factory for development and reloading. It sounds like a wacky plan today, but 90 years ago it worked wonders—for a while. And it opened up innumerable new business opportunities: neighborhood development labs, home darkroom equipment, snapshot albums, the little black doodads that you glue into albums to hold snapshots by their corners, different films for different uses, cameras with interchangeable lenses, filters, shoulder bags for the proliferating variety of photo equipment—limitless new opportunities for the Eastman Kodak Corporation itself, for its competitors, for local merchants, for stationery and luggage manufacturers and retailers, and so forth.

An innovation does not have to deserve mention in the history books to be effective. A business does not have to grow into an international colossus like Eastman Kodak to be successful. There are even businesses that succeed for a long time by doing exactly the same thing in almost exactly the same way year after year. But sooner or later, changes in the world around them will force even these fixtures of stability to innovate or die.

Whatever his situation and no matter how lofty or how modest his goals, the small businessman must amplify and clarify his business definition by using his most basic resource, creativity. The keys to an effective strategic approach are these four tools: differentiation and concentration, nondirect confrontation, challenging conventional assumptions, and constantly looking for new directions of opportunity. All of these tools involve studying the segments of the market and breaking through or reversing the impact of the "inhibitors" discussed earlier in this chapter. Instead of limiting himself through a reliance on traditional thinking patterns, the effective venturer uses an understanding of those patterns to go beyond them.

SUGGESTED READINGS

De Bono, Edward. *Lateral Thinking*. New York: Harper & Row, 1974.

Fisher, Milton. *Intuition*. New York: E. P. Dutton, 1981.

Mitchell, Arnold. *The Nine American Lifestyles*. New York: Macmillan, 1983.

Moody, Paul. *Decision Making*. New York: McGraw-Hill, 1983.

Ohmae, Kenichi. *The Mind of the Strategist*. New York: McGraw-Hill, 1982.

Pascale, Richard Tanner, and Anthony G. Athos. *The Art of Japanese Management*. New York: Simon & Schuster, 1981.

Porter, Michael E. *Competitive Strategy: Techniques for Analyzing Industries and Competitors*. New York: Free Press, 1980.

Shook, Robert L. *Why Didn't I Think of That?* New York: New American Library, 1982.

Von Oech, Roger. *A Whack on the Side of the Head*. New York: Warner Books, 1983.

Yavitz, Boris, and William H. Newman. *Strategy in Action*. New York: Free Press, 1982.

4 An approach to marketing

When one accepts the fact that the definition of a business must have a market orientation, must focus on the consumer, it follows logically that the entire structure of the business must have the marketing concept as its foundation. As we have pointed out, it is only the successful completion of the marketing function that creates sales, and it is only the creation of sales that leads to profits. All other functions of the business—manufacturing, administration, purchasing—only create costs. No matter how successful a business is in any of these subsidiary functions, unless its marketing effort is effective, the business will only succeed in building some form of inventory.

THE PARTS OF THE MARKETING TASK AND THEIR INTERRELATION

The marketing task can be divided into five different parts:

1. Designing the product or service.
2. Identifying and quantifying the market.
3. Developing the potential consumer's awareness that a response to his (conscious or unconscious) need exists.
4. Making the product or service accessible to the consumer.
5. Enticing the consumer.

While these five parts of the marketing task each deserve separate consideration, in the planning phase they must be approached simultaneously. All the aspects of the marketing program are intimately related. In fact, *the totality of the marketing mix is the product or service* in the eyes of the consumer. The five parts of the marketing task together form the means of strategy implementation. They are the package of satisfaction that meets the consumer's need.

DESIGNING THE PRODUCT

This point becomes clear as we talk about the design of the product. Marketing research defines the manifestation of the consumer need; it tells us what the consumer considers important; it gives us the shape of the offering. As discussed in the previous chapter, the selected strategy can dictate that the service aspect of the product is to be of prime importance to the proposed enterprise—anything from initial delivery time to repair policy, from availability to training, from guarantees to instruction. The combination of product and service that the business offers becomes what Theodore Levitt refers to as the "amplified product." In the same sense, marketing research may reveal that status appeals—self-esteem and the esteem of others—are the product needs of prime importance to the targeted customer. In that case, such considerations as location, decor, name, price, and advertising become significant factors in product design. Once we acknowledge that product differentiation is the major strategic opportunity for small business, it becomes obvious that all elements of business policy are part of the marketing mix that must contribute to the dictates of the specified differentiation.

The costs of the diverse elements of the marketing package must be considered as basic to the cost of the product, and each of these costs must meet a sales-producing standard to justify itself. As we have said earlier, a particular expense is valid only if the customer is willing to pay for what it produces. In a very real sense, the customer's response to the "amplified product" is more significant than his response to the *generic product*, the thing itself. The elements distinguishing one product or service from another come from a series of strategic decisions that give the generic item an identity. While each of the costs that flow from these decisions may be a separate consideration for the producer, the decisions and the resultant merchandising mix represent the "amplified" version of the generic product to the consumer, the only way in which he sees the product or service.

Consider the brokerage firm selling IBM stock. The generic product is identical, no matter which brokerage firm sells it. And yet each brokerage firm attempts to develop an identity that amplifies the product in the eyes of the consumer. Merrill Lynch doesn't sell IBM—it sells Merrill Lynch IBM. Its offering of the stock is differentiated in a particular way—by expertise, availability, and so on. Similarly, an automobile is not a collection of parts that has the capacity to transport something but a collection of value satisfactions that are mixed together in an effort to entice the consumer. Each automobile manufacturer chooses the value satisfactions that it wishes to emphasize and markets its total product accordingly. Thus James L. Schorr of Holiday Inns, Inc., says, "What I am really selling...is a hotel experience," and goes on to decide which aspects of that experience are most important to the travelers he wishes to attract.[1]

An interesting illustration of this point is a recent promotion by the manufacturer of a designer-licensed apparel product. This manufacturer enjoyed enormous success with a particular item of apparel that bore the label of a well-known fashion personality. One of his major retailers requested a quantity of these items at a special price for his annual one-third-off promotion. The manufacturer pointed out that his contractual arrangement with the designer prohibited merchandise carrying the designer label from being offered for price promotions. However, in order to retain the retailer's goodwill, the manufacturer agreed to provide at a lower price several hundred units identical in all respects to the original merchandise, but without the designer label. When this merchandise was offered for sale at one third less than the normal retail price, the promotion was unsuccessful. Obviously, the designer label was worth something to both the manufacturer and the consumer.

As discussed in Chapter 3, the choice of the element or elements to be emphasized represents the strategic approach to the market, management's assumptions concerning the probabilities of consumer response.

Price is the cost of the various assumptions. The allowable price will often depend on how many of the marketing functions the customer is willing to allow the market to perform for her. Delivered products, charged products, and more easily available products all involve additional costs, but the customer may perceive such products as being worth more. The product that the consumer perceives as coming

---

[1]The subject of "relationship marketing" is illustrative here. Relationship marketing deals with the need for continuous dialogue with the purchaser *after* the sale is made. It is no doubt the most overlooked part of the marketing mix. In those cases where the possibility of repeat business exists, the maintenance of a sincerely concerned dialogue with the purchaser provides the glue that keeps the buyer-seller relationship intact. Examples of such dialogue include telephone inquiries concerning customer satisfaction, information on opportunities for improvement of the purchased product, and birthday cards for Cabbage Patch dolls. Such efforts can be expensive, and when the businessman evaluates their potential and decides that they are appropriate, they must be costed on the same basis as any other ingredient of the marketing mix.

closest to her total needs is the product that she will purchase. The need for lesser costs may, of course, outweigh other needs of the customer.

A subsidiary point necessary to understand this process of need satisfaction is the concept of risk avoidance—the other side of the purchasing coin. The decision to purchase a product involves the risk of unsatisfactory performance as well as possible social, psychological, and physical risks. The higher the purchase price and the more significant the expected use, the greater is the perceived risk. Thus a response to the problem of risk avoidance is a necessary product component at certain price levels. At those levels, the job of the marketer is to determine the relative importance of each appeal to his targeted consumer.

We have already related the purpose of the business enterprise to the task of satisfying a need (or raising it to the level of a conscious decision). When you design and develop a product or service, it is necessary to place that product or service somewhere in the need scale in order to develop a workable approach to being in business.

IDENTIFYING AND QUANTIFYING THE MARKET

Various approaches can be used to locate the need or want that the venturer chooses to satisfy, and there are a number of ways to predict the "demand schedule," the degree of potential consumer response to the consequent product or service. As we have shown, it is of great importance in this connection to remember that the product or service we are offering is a reply to a combination of psychological wants and sociological and demographic trends, and an evaluation of the potential demand must include an analysis of these elements.

Product differentiation

While each of these wants and trends may vary in degree of importance for a particular product, establishing the numbers and the identifiable characteristics of the target group is the first element in the marketing effort and the major determinant of the marketing strategy. To succeed in his marketing effort, the small businessman must determine that the specific need that he proposes to satisfy is not already being satisfied *in the way in which he intends to satisfy it*—that his solution to the perceived problem is distinctive. This is the imperative of the strategy of product differentiation. For example, if his enterprise is intended to satisfy the needs of home improvement "do-it-yourselfers," the small businessman must determine either that there are not enough enterprises already servicing this need within the target area, or he must come up with an approach to the need that the potential customer will perceive as more effective than the approaches already being offered.

The following matrix is another way of looking at this situation:

	Existing product	Modified product	New product
Existing market	A	B	C
Identifiable market	D	E	F
Unknown market	G	H	I

Remember, the product or service as defined in this situation is the complete idea that you are offering, the total presentation of your idea. Your probability of success will differ according to the box you choose and the individual factors at play within it. If, for example, you choose Box A, if your product or service is perceived as the same as one that is already available to meet a particular need (existing need), your chances of success will depend largely on the degree of demand. If within your target area long lines of people are waiting to purchase the product or service from the already existing sources, your probability of success is good. If, on the other hand, the existing sources are barely managing to survive, your probability of success is not good.

Remember again, however, that we are defining the product or service as the total presentation. The old-line "takeout" delicatessen is not the same service as the gourmet, prepared foods store. The charge account, home delivery grocery store is not the same service as the supermarket. There are different demand schedules here; different people are willing to pay different amounts for these different services because the services involved meet different needs. Compare a "no frills" food store with a food store that is open 24 hours a day and offers home delivery and charge accounts. Even if the merchandise of the two stores is exactly the same—Heinz ketchup, for example—their pricing schedules must be different because they are offering two different packages. However, the question for the businessman is always whether consumers place the same cost value on the elements of product differentiation as he does—whether, for example, consumers feel that convenient location is worth what it costs. This kind of determination is at the heart of small business. Because the current competitive environment offers the consumer such a huge variety of choices, the marketer must move with a sure step.

Are the food entrepreneurs behind two differentiated services in competition? Of course. Everyone who is in business is in competition with everyone else in business because the market lacks sufficient financial means to satisfy all of its possible demands. The fashion retailer competes with the travel agent, and the skill with which he stimulates the need for his service will determine his success among all those bidding for the dollar.[2] Many years ago, the Harvard economist John Galbraith stated that in the United States it's not a question of baking the pie but of how it will be divided. It is not good enough for the small businessman to gain a share of the market—he must also be certain that the market he shares is large enough to support the viable, differentiated entries. By focusing on basic needs and developing a sensitivity to change, the good manager enables his business to survive and grow. Although this point may seem obvious, it is often ignored.

Marketing research

There are two equally valid approaches to the identification and quantification of demand. One starts with the idea for a product or service; the other focuses on convergent market variables and then isolates an emergent requirement. More simply stated, we can start with either the product (the solution) or the need (the problem). Regardless of where we begin, the subsequent steps are the same because in both cases the assumptions intrinsic to the idea must be tested. It matters little whether the idea for a gourmet takeout food service developed because a businessperson felt that he had a particular skill in the area

[2] An explanation of why we have not distinguished product marketing from service marketing is in order here. Although there are differences between the two, such as the greater difficulties of the service businesses in maintaining quality control and the lesser ability of the service industries to meet more immediate demand requirements through inventorying, the major difference usually cited contrasts the tangible nature of products with the intangible quality of services. However, as the nation becomes more affluent, as the number of choices for financial commitment widens and as products and services become more sophisticated, the intangible qualities of products and services take on relatively greater importance, and the distinction between the marketing of products and the marketing of services thus becomes blurred.

of food preparation or because he focused on such factors as the growing number of working women, the rising affluence of the baby-boom generation, or changing food habits. The idea must still be tested against the sociology and demographics of the particular geographic market and then quantified and evaluated. Because the product is the totality of the market's effect, the idea that is to be tested must come after a series of calculated assumptions have been made. There is little value to the question "What do you think of a gourmet takeout food store?" unless you deal with the other aspects of your marketing program: located where? with or without delivery? open when? selling what? at what prices?

The degree and the methodology of the marketing research will depend on the scope of the prospective enterprise. On the statistical level, there is an unbelievable amount of accessible information ranging from personal inspection of physical areas to census data accumulated and refined by such agencies as the Data Service affiliated with *Sales Management* magazine. Such data are of primary importance, however, only after the target consumer has been defined.

An interesting example of such a definition appears in a study on solar products conducted by Barbara Farhar-Pilgram and Charles T. Unseld. Starting with the fact that the market for residential solar products was expanding rapidly, the researchers set out to target the customer. After compiling a list of 6,144 residential users from directories provided by researchers, solar energy centers, state and local energy offices and societies, and inquiries generated by press releases sent to various publications, they designed a questionnaire that brought a 62 percent response. Among other pertinent facts, the response to the questionnaire revealed that the current owners of solar homes were middle-aged, well educated, and politically conservative—two out of three were between 35 and 64; two thirds were college graduates; nearly 40 percent had attended graduate school; and 42 percent labeled themselves politically conservative. Proficiency in carpentry, car repair, and food preservation was claimed by a majority of the respondents. One in four of them rode bicycles; 49 percent recycled newspapers.

Other methods of defining and characterizing the consumer to be targeted have been discussed in Chapter 3. (See the summary of Maggie Fine's attitude survey and Phillip Meyer's psychographic study.)

Armed with such research, it becomes relatively easy to test a new idea in the field, either through personal observation or through various types of surveys.

But research, no matter how good, can only obtain the answers to questions. Thus its quality is directly proportional to the skill with which the questions are chosen and framed, regardless of the scope and size of the research effort.[3]

A man who operated a refrigerator repair service had a particular problem, namely, that the typical refrigerator needed service only once in every seven years. While it was easy enough to identify potential customers (everyone who owned a refrigerator was a potential customer), how was he to find active customers? He developed his answer by questioning 10 women, 8 of whom told him that the last time they sought such a service they consulted the Yellow Pages. By then determining that what attracted them in the Yellow Pages was the first service listed that specified the relevant brand in its advertisement, he designed a new marketing strategy—a listing under AA mentioning all the major brands. By retaining his earlier listing (Peerless), he was able to monitor the success of the new strategy.

The questions asked by the marketing research should produce answers that include information on the degree (strong or weak) of response to the total product idea; the characteristics (age, sex, education, etc.), location, and size of the market that is of direct concern to the venturer; the most important aspects of the product; feelings about price; media awareness (how attention can be brought to the idea); and where the consumer is most likely to purchase the service or product. The determination of the qualities and needs that distinguish one potential user from another is the central concern of marketing research that seeks a path to differentiation.[4] The depth of response with which questions must be answered will vary tremendously with the product or service. The realistic business operation must always keep in mind that while an almost infinite amount of business information is available, it is time-consuming and expensive to generate and analyze information. Selectivity is the key to efficiency. (See Table 4–1 for guidelines on the design of a marketing research questionnaire and a sample questionnaire.)

---

[3]Two major difficulties in the marketing research area involve the objectivity of the interview and the receptivity of the entrepreneur. Although it seems obvious that the purpose of marketing research is not to prove the entrepreneur's assumptions but to test them, in some instances research has been conducted as though the opposite were true. Once the objectives of a research project are determined, *listening* is the skill involved.

[4]An interesting subject arises under the subject of "heavy users." In many products or services, there is a disproportionate balance among consumers. For example, 14 percent of all gin drinkers consume 80 percent of all the gin purchased; 23 percent of all laxative users consume 80 percent of all the laxatives used; 32 percent of all beer drinkers drink 80 percent of all the beer bought. Concentration on the heavy user—or, as the airlines call him, "the frequent traveler"—can be particularly cost effective. By determining the characteristics of the heavy user, it is possible to develop an extremely efficient marketing effort.

TABLE 4–1 Designing a marketing research questionnaire

1. The basic information should be filled in before the interview. The questionnaire should be designed with simple, nonpersonal information first, becoming increasingly complicated and personal.
2. The earliest parts should be stated by the interviewer in his own words and should be used as a method of establishing rapport with the subject.
3. The product description should be informational. It should not be imparted in a "selling" way. The interviewer should avoid the tendency to produce product-biased answers.
4. The presumed product appeals, including price, must be tested by the questionnaire. The assumptions should be presented to the interviewee for his reaction.
5. The interviewee's buying intentions at various price points should be determined. Perhaps a demand curve can be constructed. If the interviewee's intention is not to buy, clues to his reasoning should be sought as a guide to possible product or service correction.
6. Retail outlets and advertising media should be explored.
7. Avoid specific questions relative to age and income.

Sample Questionnaire

Name of respondent ______________ Name of interviewer ______________
Address ______________ Date ______________
Phone ______________ Time ______________
Other (nonpersonal) relevant data ______________

Good morning. My name is ______________, and I am conducting a marketing study for a new product (service) called ______________. The answers you give to the following questions will help determine whether or not to introduce this new product (service) idea and what features to incorporate into the product. May I have a few minutes of your time?

The name of this product is ______________. It is a ______________, and it functions (purposes) are ______________
______________.

The benefits of this product are ______________
______________.

1. What is your immediate reaction to this idea?

Positive	**Negative**
Great ________	So-so ________
Like it very much ________	Do not particularly like it ________
Like it somewhat ________	Do not like it at all ________

Why do you say that? Explain. ______________
____
____

TABLE 4–1 ***(concluded)***

2. Which of the following best expresses your feeling about buying this product if it were available to you?

Positive	**Negative**
I'm absolutely sure I would buy it ________	I probably would not buy it ________
I'm almost sure I would buy it ________	I'm almost sure I would not buy it ________
I probably would buy it ________	I'm absolutely sure I would not buy it ________

Why do you say that? ____

____

____

3. All things considered, what is there about this product idea that appeals to you most. What do you consider its most important advantages?

Appeal	**Advantages**
1. ____________________	1. ____________________
2. ____________________	2. ____________________
3. ____________________	3. ____________________

4. How much do you think such a product would cost? ________________
5. Where would you expect to buy such a product? ________________
6. Where would you expect such a product to be advertised? ________________
7. Are there any suggestions you would care to make that you think might improve this product? ____

   ____

Classification data:

1. In which category does your age fall:		2. Please tell me where you total family income falls:	
Under 15	________________	Below $5,000	________________
16–21	________________	$5,000–9,999	________________
22–29	________________	$10,000–14,999	________________
30–49	________________	$15,000–20,000	________________
50–60	________________	Above $20,000	________________
Over 60	________________		

3. Check one:

Female:	Single ______________	Married ______________
Male:	Single ______________	Married ______________

Thank you for your cooperation.

Statistical measurement follows once the characteristics of the target audience have been developed and refined. In the solar products and refrigerator repair service cases, the numbers were evident. Statistical analysis can range from counting the traffic at a particular location to using the information provided by the U.S. Census Bureau. The time, effort, and money that the small businessman spends on identifying and quantifying the target group depends on the skill and ingenuity with which this task is performed, so it should be carefully thought out. Direct interviews, easily purchased mailing lists, directories, trade magazines, voter lists, and reply coupons in advertising or as product enclosures can all be helpful. *The more you know about your customers, the easier it is to identify and quantify them.* New data base services are springing up daily.

DEVELOPING AN AWARENESS AMONG POTENTIAL CONSUMERS

Developing an awareness among your potential consumers that a response to their need exists is a science that ranges from creating a clear, readable sign to a national television advertising campaign.

The components of the awareness effort

This awareness effort has four essential components: advertising, public relations, sales promotion, and personal selling, and the balance between these components varies by the type of market, the knowledge of the buyer, and the resources of the seller. In his book *Marketing Management*, Philip Kotler expresses it as shown in Figures 4–1 and 4–2.

As Figure 4–1 shows, for consumer products, advertising and sales promotion are normally the largest components of the "awareness budget." The more a product or service must be differentiated, the greater is the need for personal selling. The narrower the market, the smaller is the proportion of the awareness budget required for advertising and the larger is the proportion required for personal selling. An overstatement is illustrative: if the service is designed for one person, the *Reader's Digest* is not an effective awareness instrument.

Figure 4–2 shows that, as awareness grows in the market, the consumer moves from comprehension to conviction to ordering and personal selling takes on an ever greater role.

The blending of the generic product and the appeal is the product image. This is the central concept of marketing, and because, as we

FIGURE 4–1 Distribution of the awareness budget in the sale of consumer products and industrial and trade products

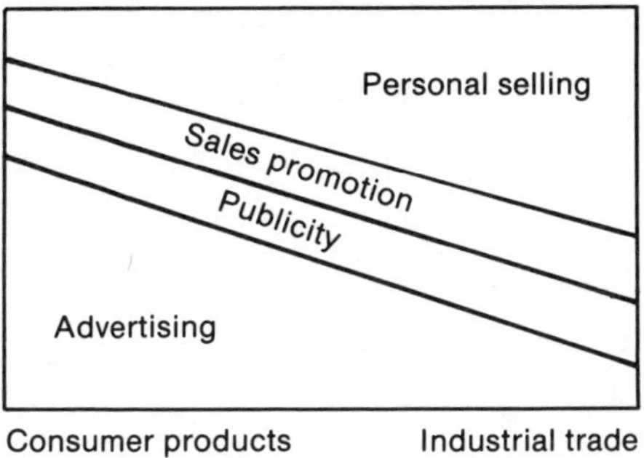

Source: Philip Kotler, *Marketing Management: Analysis, Planning, and Control*, 4th ed., © 1980, p. 481. Reprinted by permission of Prentice-Hall, Inc. Englewood Cliffs, N.J.

FIGURE 4–2 Shifts in the awareness budget with increasing awareness

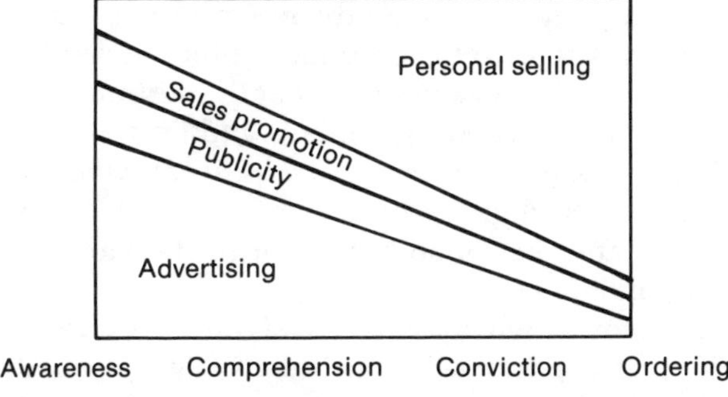

Source: Philip Kotler, *Marketing Management: Analysis, Planning, and Control*, 4th ed., © 1980, p. 481. Reprinted by permission of Prentice-Hall, Inc. Englewood Cliffs, N.J.

have stated, the product *is* the total marketing mix, we again emphasize that each aspect of product development, including the awareness effort, must be consistent with the desired perception. The product image is the blend of product stimuli projected to the consumer. It includes the company name, the product or service name, the logo, the package, the decor, the uniform, and the telephone voice—all the things that send a message, that contribute to the product image.

Consider the name of a simple object, for example:

Source: Anne Anastasia, *Fields of Applied Psychology* (New York: McGraw-Hill, 1979), p. 295.

One of these objects is called Lamolay, and the other is called Taratok. Almost everyone agrees that Lamolay is on the left.

The purpose of the product logo or trademark is to serve as a conditioned stimulus for the recall of the product and the company name. The aggressive company will take advantage of opportunities to use the logo or trademark to help the customer build the desired bridges to its product or service. Such values as strength, desirability, reliability, and freshness can be suggested by symbols and by words. This idea is particularly important in the pure service business, where the intangible qualities of the offering far outweigh its tangible qualities. The Prudential "rock," and the "good hands" of Allstate are tangible symbols that sell intangible services.

The company name itself may have a significant effect on marketing success. This is illustrated by the case of Spectrum Pictures, an audio-video film production company that was seeking entry into the field of training films. As Spectrum Pictures, its effort to identify potential customers was unsuccessful. As Spectrum Communications, its effort to find companies with communication problems enabled the young firm to turn the corner. Messages left by Spectrum Communications were remembered.

Sometimes a simple line, a slogan, can also do wonders.

A very successful public relations campaign was devised years ago by the PR genius Ben Sonnenberg for a major food processor. At that time (some 50 years ago), all of the tuna on the market was pink. However, the tuna processed by Sonnenberg's client was white—and therefore not salable. Sonnenberg created the line "Guaranteed not to turn pink in the can." Used on all of its cans, boxes, advertising, and stationery, that line turned around the company's fortunes.

The small businessman should not overlook any possible aspect of the awareness effort. Bulletin boards, circulars, brochures, personal letters, and signs can all be utilized at minimal cost. The efficiency of the awareness effort is of crucial concern for the small businessman because, while it is commonly conceded that the awareness aspects of the product mix are important, spending nonproductive money on those aspects is very easy. If, for example, your target audience is a woman possessing certain clearly identifiable characteristics, how do you eliminate the balance of the population from your advertising costs? What is the best way for the refrigeration repairman to reach his market? When the business operation approaches the task of reaching its target audience intelligently, through research, minimizing nonproductive awareness costs sometimes becomes easier. If the refrigeration repairman finds that most of the people seeking the services he offers consult the Yellow Pages, he only has to find out what features characterize a successful Yellow Page ad—position, size, brand names, and so on. Mock-up pages can easily be prepared and tested by even the smallest entrepreneur. Within certain limitations, advertising can and should be approached scientifically. Beautiful graphics do not make a good ad any more than neat counters make a good sale. The best newspaper or magazine for a particular company is not necessarily the paper that the entrepreneur likes. The point to remember is that advertising is a part of the product as well as an attention-getting device. When effective, it offers the promise of a solution to a problem. When you are investigating your awareness devices, you must know who your target audience is and enough about *her* living habits to reach *her* in the simplest, most efficient way.

Advertising

Advertising, whether it is aimed at the trade or the consumer, is expensive for the small business and should be considered carefully. It can achieve several objectives:

1. It can develop sales leads and soften up the buyer.
2. It can explain the new features or the unique qualities of the product.
3. It can legitimate the product and the company.
4. It can reinforce the positioning effort.
5. It can create sales.

Because it is very easy to spend great amounts of money on advertising without having an accurate measure of its effectiveness (there is terrific "ego" temptation in advertising), the objectives of an advertising effort and a particular series of ads should be written out by the business operator. These should include a full statement of who the target is, what the need is, what the solution is, and what the specific message is. As David Ogilvy puts it, "What promise would be most likely to make them buy your brand?" The more simply and definitely this promise can be stated, the more effective the advertisement is. Ogilvy's "six reasons why you should buy" advertisement clearly exemplifies this principle, and the idea has validity whether it is expressed or implied.

And the question "Is there a cheaper, more effective way to deliver the message?" should always be raised. Here the inhibitors to creativity discussed in the previous chapter should be reviewed. Is the advertising the first solution or the best solution?

The accompanying commonly accepted advertising rules have been formulated by Ogilvy and others. (Exceptions to these rules can and should be made.)

A few advertising rules

1. The most effective stimuli arouse some emotional response. Good advertising tells a story that involves the viewer.
2. The headlines that work best promise the reader a benefit. Knowledge of results leads to increases in recall. Illustrate the results where possible.
3. If the materials to be remembered are different or unique, they work better.
4. Advertising is most effective when it calls for minimal attitude change. Concentrate on the most likely users.
5. Creditability is important, but over a period of time the use of well-known figures for testimonials is no more effective than the use of unknowns with whom the viewer can identify. When you put headlines in quotes, you increase recall substantially.
6. Headlines that contain news are especially effective. The use of "amazing," "introducing," "now," and "suddenly" works.
7. Continuous repetition of a message, of an identical ad, is effective.
8. Five times as many people read the headline as read the body copy.
9. The viewer sees the ad alone. Think of him individually.
10. It's the viewer who has to impressed, not you. Keep it personal, simple, understandable.
11. Look for Ogilvy's "big idea"—the unique approach that fits the strategy perfectly, that can be used for 30 years, that produces a "wow" when you think about it.

Public relations

For new businesses or new products within an existing business, public relations and sales promotion can be the most cost-effective road toward success. The Hula-Hoop, the Slinky, and the Frisbee sat quietly on the shelf until they were actually demonstrated in retail stores and on playing fields. Local newspapers and television are less difficult to break into than one might expect, provided that a legitimate and interesting story can be developed. There is obviously a gap between the professional approach to public relations and the amateur's efforts, but frequently the enthusiasm of the amateur can bridge this gap. This is another area that offers a great premium for creativity, with special dividends for just hard work.

The field of public relations must be viewed in exactly the same way as the simple product or the advertising. The key is to develop an innovative, attention-getting method of illustrating a response to a need. (It is relevant to note that the various media have a need too—filling space in an interesting way. The astute PR person deals directly with that need.)

As we pointed out in Chapter 3, the individual firm has a host of interested observers in its competitive environment, and effective public relations can have a "strategic" impact on any or all of them. In certain business situations—when particular components are in short supply or when credit is hard to obtain—a campaign aimed at suppliers may be more important than one aimed at consumers. In other situations, a public relations campaign aimed at the competition may accomplish an important objective.

Public relations is probably the least expensive element of the marketing mix. It can be very effective because of the involvement of the so-called third party in the relationship between the company and its target. This third party—most often the media—contributes both credibility and the "soft sell," both of which are difficult to achieve through the other awareness avenues.

Trade publications are a relatively simple public relations option. The better the story, the better the exposure. Trade publications use almost every photograph submitted if it conforms to their technical requirements. Direct mail done in the form of newsletters, especially when pertinent outside information is included, often conveys as much credibility as do the legitimate media. The possibilities in public relations are limited only by the creativity of the originator.

Sales promotion

Sales promotion is particularly important to a small business because it can lead directly to the success story for which other potential buyers are waiting. It is the most effective short-range weapon in the arsenal. Any purchase incentive—coupons, gift with purchase, cooperative advertising, and so on—should be considered here. Which one is used depends on the exact effect that the marketer is trying to create. Properly executed sales promotion gives the product or service visibility, and in the world of illusion, visibility confers credibility. The retailer, for example, may view five requests for a specific product as an avalanche of demand.

Personal selling

Although the title of the salesperson varies from situation to situation—both the gallery attendant and the traveling sales representative are salespersons—the task of the salesperson remains the same: to relate the company's services to the customer's needs.

The closer the company's control over its salespeople, the greater are the chances for effectiveness. (The motivational factors involved are discussed in Chapter 8.) Given a choice between salespeople who work exclusively for one company and the independent sales agents who represent a number of firms, there is no question that if the potential sales warrant the expense, the company person will perform the intermediate and long-range sales functions best. The trade-offs to be considered in making the choice are, on the one hand, the need for short-range introductory successes that may be more easily obtained by the experienced multiproduct salesperson through his established contacts and, on the other hand, the amount of time that may be necessary to explain and introduce a new service, time that the established salesperson may be unwilling to spend. For the new business, the fixed-costs aspects of the salaried salesperson may be the determining factor in the choice, but, as we will discuss in Chapter 6, extreme caution should be exercised in determining which strategic tools are sacrificed for financial reasons.

Generally speaking, the personnel who make up the sales organization, the selling people on the department store floor or the sales agents, seem to be the company resource that is used least effectively. This is no doubt caused by preoccupation with the product or service as opposed to the more significant marketing orientation that we have been discussing. A clear understanding by the sales organization of the management message and how it is to be conveyed to the consumer is central to operational effectiveness. Achieving such an understanding is a crucial, ongoing management responsibility. Similarly, the sales organization should be viewed as a source of important feedback to the company, though many companies have a "shoot the messenger carrying the bad news" attitude.

Strange as it may seem, the conventional small business frequently sees salespeople as separate from the product or service. This is particularly ironic in the direct service business (as opposed to the packaged goods business, for example), where face-to-face interaction between the company and the consumer is often the essential quality of the offering. Retailing is a prime offender in this regard, but there are others. (It is interesting to note that, unlike its long-established department store competitors, Nordstrom's, an innovative and highly successful West Coast retailer, pays its salespeople more than it pays its merchandisers.)

While there are a great number of compensation schemes for salespeople, management should consider the proper balance between salary and commission within the framework of the competitive strategies discussed in Chapter 3. What it takes to do the job should be the determining factor. Specific aspects of the company's marketing plan can be tied to particular sales incentives to provide extra emphasis. Extra compensation for developing elements of the company's differentiated market thrust can assure the desired image projection.

In businesses where there are intermediate consumers—retailers of the company's product or service—the businessman must be particularly careful to establish a proper perspective. He should understand that, although these secondary consumers are essentially channels of distribution to the real consumer, they must be viewed with the same type of thinking that is applicable to the ultimate consumer—the product or service must be seen in terms of the retailers' needs and wants.

The significant perceived need of the retailer is the need for profit. Each dollar that the retailer invests in space and personnel must be utilized to earn a return on that investment. The manufacturer or wholesaler who can offer a better return on the retailer's investment becomes an important resource. This return can result either from direct sales of the product or from the traffic that the product brings into the store. But the sales and traffic must be translatable into bottom line dollars, preferably in the short run. *All decisions relating to the retail structure must be viewed from this perspective.* It is the logical extension of the "Everyone operates in his own self-interest" theorem, and while it is often shortsighted, it must be accepted as an unavoidable fact of life.

The manufacturer or wholesaler who depends on the retailer as a channel of distribution to the consumer must give the retailer an incentive to allocate the necessary amount of space to his product. This relates specifically to the profit (gross margin percentage) that the businessman allows the retailer to make as well as to the actual dollars that the businessman attracts to the retailer through efforts to build traffic volume. Techniques that can help in this regard range from the assumption of certain selling costs to national advertising. The sales promotion techniques that can be helpful include innovative and relatively inexpensive programs such as trunk shows, demonstrations, and personal appearances and such devices as the purchase-with-purchase and gift-with-purchase programs that have been used used so successfully in the cosmetics industry.

The manufacturer or wholesaler who is involved with the retail structure must carefully distinguish between similar but markedly different types of retailers. It is considerably more expensive to deal with the traditional retail outlets such as department stores than it is to deal with the new promotional discount stores. At the moment, the traditional retail outlets require considerably more in terms of support from their vendors and are impervious to the costs of that support. The discounters, on the other hand, perhaps because they are offering less in terms of service, demand less from the support structure. Using our basic concept again here, we see that when the traditional retailer buys a product, he is indeed buying the total marketing package. The manufacturer or wholesaler must view the retailer, the secondary consumer, not as an adversary, but as an adjunct of his own operation, and he must be certain that his marketing effort takes the needs and costs of this channel into careful consideration when he designs his marketing package. The retailer, on the other hand, must view his vendor relationship in the same way, explaining to his sources of supply what he needs from them and in turn doing whatever he can to contribute to the health of a cooperative supplier. The success of any business enterprise depends in large part on the health of its supply structure.

MAKING THE PRODUCT ACCESSIBLE AND ENTICING

The approaches to the "availability" aspect of the marketing program are also interrelated with the other elements of the strategic package. These approaches derive essentially from how the marketer evaluates the need he is dealing with and from how that need manifests itself. The distinction is normally made between "convenience" products and "specialty" products, between products that consumers will buy if and when it is convenient and products that consumers are willing to make a special effort to buy. The former are usually inexpensive and frequently purchased; the latter are expensive and are bought only on special occasions. The selection of the various marketing tools, from location to packaging, will vary greatly according to where the product or service falls on the convenience-specialty scale. Marketing decisions must be viewed in that light rather than as abstractions.

The effort to make the package enticing is of course implied throughout the marketing program, and the effectiveness of that effort depends on how clearly the problem and solution are spelled out. In the case of the Hula-Hoop, the initial enticement message—that it was great fun—could best be delivered by demonstration. In the case of a hemorrhoid preparation, the enticement message of the print advertising was "Send a dollar, relieve the pain—keep the dollar, keep the pain." The message worked. If the product or service answers a real need in a distinctive and differentiated way, the essence of the enticement is inherent. The means of projecting that enticement must therefore flow from that basic quality. It must be viewed in the problem/solution context—who is interested and why, what does he or she require, and how can we best touch that need.

SUGGESTED READINGS

Cohen, William A., and Marshall E. Reddick. *Successful Marketing for Small Business*. New York: AMACOM, 1981.

Culligan, Matthew J., and Dolph Greene. *Getting Back to the Basics of Public Relations and Personality*. New York: Crown Publishers, 1982.

Kotler, Philip. *Marketing Management*. 4th ed. Englewood Cliffs, N.J.: Prentice-Hall, 1980.

Levinson, Jay Conrad. *Guerilla Marketing*. Boston: Houghton Mifflin, 1984.

Lovelock, Christopher. *Services Marketing*. Englewood Cliffs, N.J.: Prentice-Hall, 1984.

Nash, Edward L. *Direct Marketing*. New York: McGraw-Hill, 1982.

Ogilvy, David. *Ogilvy on Advertising*. New York: Crown Publishers, 1983.

5 Techniques of planning, control, and evaluation

The use of numbers is an integral part of business management because numbers provide a simply understood frame of reference for planning and appraising performance. While numbers in themselves are meaningless (1,000, for example, means nothing), the accounting requirement that they be expressed in monetary terms—dollars or similar references—allows businesspeople to converse in a universally understood language that can be understood by persons with a minimal financial background. Because numbers enable the manager and other participants in the business dialogue to move away from vague generalities—"Business is good (bad)"; "It's expensive"—the task of running a business assumes a workable form.

As already mentioned, the most common trap that small business operators fall into is that they adopt a product orientation rather than a business orientation. Most small business owners, particularly venturers in new businesses, are so involved in what they are producing that they tend to be uninterested in numbers. As a result, they develop little sophistication in their use and thus fail to utilize the various planning, controlling, and evaluating documents effectively. This is a serious mistake. When financial planning techniques are viewed objectively, they are neither mysterious nor complicated. Mastery of these vital tools is well within the competence of the average person.

While it is frequently difficult to assign a dollar value to something (projected sales, for example), it is impossible to run a business enterprise in an orderly and intelligent manner without developing realistic estimates in the concrete terms that dollar figures require. Dollar estimates are implicit in all business decisions. For example, when a businessperson decides to advertise or to lease a particular space at a particular cost, he envisages a return on that investment. What will this expenditure do for sales volume? for profit? Effective planning requires a written commitment to that expectation in measurable terms. Yet most small businessmen are somehow unwilling to live with that written number.

FINANCIAL ACCOUNTING

The classification of business accounting information falls into two major categories. Both of these categories are important to the operator, but each has a slightly different focus. *Financial accounting* is primarily directed to the need for external evaluation. *Management accounting* is concerned primarily with the internal functions of planning, controlling, and coordination.

The balance sheet

The basic documents of financial accounting are the balance sheet and the income statement. The balance sheet provides a picture of the business at a specific moment, while the income statement indicates what occurred within the business over a specified period of time. The balance sheet is a status report, while the income statement is a description of "flow." The balance sheet is the fundamental document of the accounting cycle in that it must reflect everything that happens within the company from earnings to shifts in what it owns and what it owes, and indeed in who owns what. The income statement is more limited; in effect, it is only an explanation of earnings.

Because these items can only be expressed in dollar terms and because accounting principles require that those dollar terms be based on what the items cost a company, it is important at this point to dispel the common misconception that the balance sheet states what the company is worth (even though the owners' equity is frequently referred to as net worth). The value of a building, for example, may vary significantly from the dollar amount stated on the balance sheet. Thus what seems obvious from the use of precise numbers is not necessarily obvious.

A simple method of looking at the balance sheet separates the resources the company has (assets) from the claims of either the creditors (liabilities) or the owners (equity) against those resources.

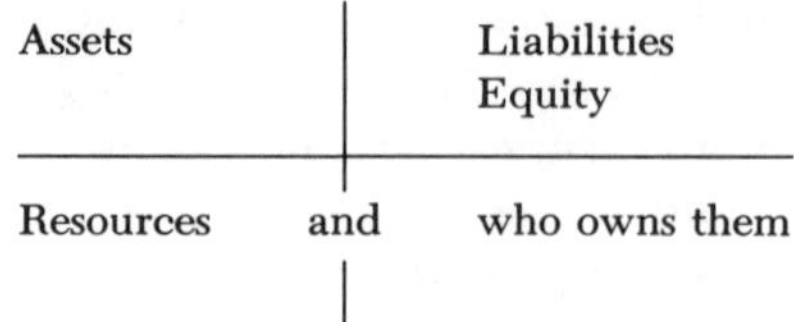

The term *balance* applies because the assets and the claims against them must balance.

Another way to view the balance sheet is to think of the left side, the asset side, as a description of how the money within the company—both the owners' money and the creditors' money—is invested. The money within the company is on the left side; the claims of the owners and the creditors are on the right side. The investment is on the left side; the investors are on the right side.

In either case, in order to qualify as an asset

1. Something must have at least the promise of an economic benefit to the company. (Something that was purchased at one time for resale and is now obsolete can no longer be listed as an asset.)
2. Its value at the time it was acquired must be objectively measurable.
3. It must be under the control of the company. (A car thus becomes an asset even if it is to be paid for in the future.)

The assets of a company, what it owns, are listed on the balance sheet in order of their liquidity—how easily they may be converted into cash.

The items on a typical balance sheet are shown in Figure 5–1.

FIGURE 5–1 Items on a typical balance sheet

Assets	Liabilities
Current assets:	Current liabilities:
Cash	Accounts payable
Marketable securities	
Accounts receivable	Salaries payable
	Accrued expenses
Inventory	Notes payable (one year)
Prepaid expenses	Estimated taxes
Fixed assets:	Long-term liabilities (more than one year):
Equipment depreciation	Debt (pay over one year)
Building depreciation	
Total assets	Equity
	Stock
	Retained earnings

Inventory (as opposed to office supplies) indicates only merchandise that has been either created or purchased with the idea of resale as part of the company's product or service offering. Paper is "inventory" to a publisher but "office supplies" to a car dealer. Similarly, an automobile is "inventory" to a car dealer but a "fixed asset" to the publisher.

A business may own two types of "intangible" assets. One type, referred to as "prepaid expenses," is the cost of future services that have already been paid for, such as insurance and rental payments. The other type, which promises benefits over a longer period of time, includes such things as patents, licenses, and goodwill. In both cases, the value of intangible assets can be stated only in terms of what they actually cost the company. The value of a patent, for example, can be either what the company paid to acquire it from another business entity or the legal costs of obtaining it if the patented item was developed internally. (The research and development costs are handled separately on the income statement as expenses in the year they were incurred.) Similarly, goodwill can be considered an asset only if the company actually paid for it. (Goodwill represents the difference between what a balance sheet shows a company is worth and the price that a purchaser pays for that company.)

The value at which assets are carried on the balance sheet may not be equivalent to the worth of those assets in the marketplace. The device by which this situation is theoretically rectified is referred to as "depreciation." It is assumed that a stipulated percentage of the value of a fixed asset—an automobile or a building, for example—is used up each year that the asset is in use.[1] When this is done, the balance sheet shows the original cost, the accumulated depreciation, and the current "value." Because this "use" is theoretical, it may leave the company with either an overstated or understated asset valuation.

"Intangible" assets are handled in much the same way, with the term *amortization* substituted for the term *depreciation*.

Current liabilities and long-term liabilities are distinguished by time. Debts payable within a year are considered current liabilities, while those payable in more than a year are continued long-term liabilities. A mortgage would be treated as both a current liability and a

---

[1] As we will note in examining the income statement, depreciation amounts to an expense without a direct cash expenditure. The amount of depreciation expense that a company is allowed to deduct annually, the number of years of theoretical usable life that an asset may be said to have, is subject to broad government control and can be used as an instrument of national economic policy. Currently, for example, in an effort to stimulate automobile sales, the government has decreed that an automobile may be considered to have an economic life of three years; one third of the cost of an automobile can thus be considered a fully deductible business expense each year. Similar policies, such as accelerated depreciation allowances and investment credit programs, are adopted from time to time for similar reasons.

long-term liability. The amount payable within a year would be a current liability; the balance would be a long-term liability.

Accrued expenses are the opposite of prepaid expenses. They include obligations of the company that do not fall within the accounts payable classification. A common example would be wages due (for work done prior to the period covered by the balance sheet but not yet paid for).

The concluding items on the balance sheet, owners' equity and retained earnings, may be used to separate the initial capital contribution (equity) and the earnings accumulated since the formation of the business.[2] For unincorporated businesses, these figures are combined under one capital account.

The balance sheet is one of the two major documents used to view a business operation from a distance. Ratios and similar statistical devices are frequently used methods of analysis.

Six ratios are considered measures of solvency or liquidity:

1. The quick ratio is computed by dividing the cash and accounts receivable by the total current liabilities. This ratio reveals the protection that short-term creditors are afforded by cash or near-cash assets. A 1-to-1 (1 : 0) ratio is considered evidence of liquidity, and the larger the ratio, obviously, the greater the liquidity.
2. The current ratio, which is obtained by dividing all current assets by all current liabilities, is an extension of the quick ratio. By including inventories and other items that are less easily collected than the so-called quick assets, it provides a slightly longer view of the company's liquidity. Here a ratio of 2 : 0 or better is normally considered good.
3. The ratio of current liabilities to inventory, like the ratio of net sales to inventory (see below), isolates the question of how dependent a company is on the inventory to meet its current obligations. Inventory must be related to sales. In a particularly seasonal business, incorrect proportions here can lead to a liquidity problem; the inventory to current liability ratio is one way to look at this situation.
4. The ratio of total liabilities to net worth measures the relationship of all debts to ownership equity. When total liabilities exceed net worth (a ratio of more than 1), the creditors have more at stake in the business than do the owners. Most banks will accept a 2-to-1 ratio.

---

[2]Where stock has been issued, a distinction may be made between the par value of the stock (the original designation of value) and what the stockholders actually paid to the company (not to be confused with the prices paid by trades on the stock market). Thus, if a stock had a par value of $1 and the stockholder actually paid the company $4, the item would appear as $1, common stock, and $4, other paid-in capital.

5. The ratio of fixed assets to net worth makes possible another judgment of where the company's assets lie. When fixed assets are particularly high in relationship to net worth (in excess of .75), this is often an indication of low working capital or overextension of funds. The fixed assets to net worth ratio is highly variable by different types of businesses.
6. The debt service coverage ratio indicates the company's ability to service its borrowings. This ratio is calculated by dividing the net profit after taxes plus depreciation by the annual principal payments plus 54 percent of the interest (the cost of the interest to the business after taxes). A good ratio here is 2 to 1, meaning that the company's cash flow is twice the amount needed to service the debt.

The income statement

The income or profit and loss statement is the second major document in the financial accounting area. In relating the revenues, the monies coming into the company, to the expenses incurred in generating those revenues, the income statement focuses on the earnings, the difference between the revenues and expenses, over a specified period.[3] This earnings or income figure then applies directly to the retained earnings item on the balance sheet. The forms in which the company has retained these earnings—inventory, cash, accounts receivable, and so forth—are noted on the left side of the balance sheet.

The two key concepts concerning revenue involve the questions of when revenue can be counted and how much to count. Revenue is considered to be realized (accountable) when a product or service is delivered, at that point in time when the product or service is invoiced. The amount of revenue realized is the amount that can reasonably be expected to be paid. Thus, for example, allowable discounts from the selling price must be provided for on the income statement.

Similarly, it is important to distinguish between costs and expenses. A cost is any expenditure made by a company. A cost or expenditure is considered an expense in terms of the income statement only when the use of the acquired resource relates to the specific accounting period covered by the income statement. A simple illustration is the purchase of a company automobile. While the purchase price is clearly a cost, only the part of the cost that the government (or standing accounting practice) considers usable within a year, the depreciable amount, can

---

[3]To avoid confusion, it is helpful to distinguish between the words *revenues* and *income*. Revenues equal all money coming in, while income, in the accounting sense, represents only the difference between revenues and expenses: Revenues − Expenses = Income.

be thought of as an expense of that year. While it is sometimes difficult in practice to make the distinction between costs and an expense, a good operating rule is that all costs are for either assets or expenses; an asset must promise future benefit, while an expense must provide current benefit.

Like revenues, costs are recognized at the moment the related product or service is received or given to a specified shipper—not when payment is required. Items for which invoices have not been received are nonetheless expenses of the given period and must be accounted for.

Typically, there are two types of income statements. The choice between them depends on how clearly one can relate the costs of a given period to the particular product or service as opposed to the more generalized costs of being in business for the specified period.

Where these two types of costs can be easily differentiated, the form is generally

  Sales
− Cost of goods sold
= Gross profit
− Operating expenses
= Net income before taxes[4]
− Taxes
= Net income after taxes

When this option is selected, the expenses that are directly related to the product or service, those that vary directly or almost directly with sales volume, are segregated and ultimately referred to as the cost of goods sold. Thus:

Sales			$10,000	
Beginning inventory		20,000		
Purchases	2,000 +			
Direct labor	2,000 +			
Freight in	200 +			
Freight out	400 +	+ 4,600		
		+ 24,600		
Closing inventory		− 20,000		
Cost of goods sold			4,600	46 %
Gross profit or gross margin			$ 5,400	54 %

[4]For differences in handling corporations, sole proprietorships, and partnerships, see Chapter 8.

This type of income statement is normally used by businesses whose ultimate product or service is based substantially on outside purchases with some degree of internal processing. The various forms of retailing and manufacturing fall into this category. While this method is inexact because of the obvious variations between the cost and the current value of inventory items—depending on the degree of obsolescence or completion—it provides a workable technique, particularly when income statements are examined sequentially over a period of time.

The second type of income statement, more common in service industries, does not attempt to separate the costs directly related to the product or service from those involved in "doing business." In such situations, the income statement avoids the categorization of cost of goods sold and might simply list[5]

= Sales
– Expenses
= Net income before taxes
– Taxes
= Net income after taxes

As we indicated at the outset, the income statement collects income by subtracting expenses from revenues. It is used primarily to evaluate performance. This is done in three ways: (1) by comparing the latest income statement with earlier statements, (2) by relating results to predetermined goals, and (3) by measuring performance against objective standards. Used in conjunction with the balance sheet, these standards may be broken down into either profitability judgments or judgments of efficiency.

Key business ratios

Six ratios are involved in efficiency measurement:

1. The collection period is determined by dividing accounts receivable by sales and multiplying the quotient by 365 days. The result should then be related to normal industry payment terms. If the normal industry payment terms, for example, are 30 days, a number exceeding that by more than a third (40 days) will indicate slow-turning receivables.
2. The net sales to inventory ratio has been discussed. By dividing annual net sales by inventory, the efficiency of the flow of funds

[5]The degree to which sales or expenses are detailed will vary with the company and with the prospective use of the income statement. A bar-restaurant, for example, might choose to break down sales by food and liquor. A business utilizing a great amount of electricity might break that expense item out separately on its income statement, while another business might classify heat, light, and electricity together.

TABLE 5–1 Selected median operating ratios, 1983–84 (Dun & Bradstreet Credit Services)

Type of business (number of firms reporting)	Net sales	Gross profit (%)	Net profit after tax (%)	Quick ratio (times)	Current ratio (times)	Current liabilities to net worth (%)	Current liabilities to inventory (%)	Total liabilities to net worth (%)	Fixed assets to net worth (%)	Collection period (days)	Sales to inventory (times)	Assets to sales (%)	Sales to net working capital (times)	Accounts payable to sales (%)	Return on sales (%)	Return on assets (%)	Return on net worth (%)
Computer programming (936)	479,000	42.6	7.4	1.4	2.0	54.4	234.5	80.3	45.9	43.8	24.3	39.9	8.2	3.2	8.7	13.0	31.3
Commercial photography (art) (645)	199,772	43.7	8.4	1.4	1.9	44.3	334.2	63.9	62.8	39.4	33.0	37.1	8.7	4.0	8.3	11.7	28.7
Direct mail adv. (102)	776,000	42.5	5.7	1.3	1.6	69.8	591.0	96.8	72.9	45.6	40.6	34.4	12.6	3.9	4.7	10.4	28.5
Beauty shops (514)	110,990	56.5	10.2	.9	2.1	18.8	137.1	33.0	77.7	8.7	29.5	30.2	11.2	1.4	10.6	19.0	27.4
Greeting card publishing (21)	540,621	42.8	7.4	1.0	2.3	67.0	74.4	93.5	25.0	38.3	4.1	55.1	3.6	3.3	5.1	8.5	24.4
Book stores (556)	196,000	33.1	5.8	.5	2.8	46.4	47.2	62.7	25.0	5.8	4.0	42.8	4.9	5.8	5.1	11.3	22.1
Eating places (1,823)	493,785	46.5	4.4	.5	1.0	47.4	437.3	97.2	106.7	4.2	61.2	32.4	20.2	2.5	4.1	8.7	22.1
Retail bakeries, baking and selling (274)	265,901	46.5	5.9	.6	1.3	38.3	243.5	78.9	103.7	3.6	43.1	25.4	21.6	1.7	6.2	12.0	21.1
Mail-order houses (362)	331,311	33.8	6.3	.8	2.2	47.5	76.3	66.5	27.4	14.6	7.0	37.5	6.1	4.2	5.5	9.9	19.3
Data procesing services (513)	900,000	45.2	5.3	1.3	1.7	56.3	644.2	99.5	76.4	39.0	52.5	46.6	9.4	3.3	5.1	8.6	19.1
Women's accessories, specialty stores (828)	132,840	36.3	6.4	.8	3.4	30.5	42.9	45.1	21.8	6.2	4.1	44.5	4.2	4.8	6.6	9.8	18.2
Drinking places, alcoholic (473)	199,019	50.9	4.9	.5	1.1	28.6	292.3	79.4	107.9	2.1	43.6	46.4	20.6	2.3	4.3	7.3	18.0

Child day care services (124)	210,000	41.6	5.9	.8	1.6	33.1	999.9	73.3	79.3	11.6	536.9	51.9	9.4	1.9	5.7	7.4	17.6
Florists (831)	180,334	45.6	5.4	1.1	2.1	37.1	122.9	61.6	58.3	22.2	14.4	36.2	9.3	3.4	4.8	9.4	16.9
Private employment agencies (198)	400,000	26.2	5.2	2.0	2.2	38.8	457.2	56.7	34.7	39.7	125.3	26.4	10.0	1.9	4.6	8.2	16.3
Hobby, toy, game stores (507)	140,000	36.8	5.1	.6	3.4	29.9	39.3	46.9	22.3	3.2	3.2	48.5	3.8	4.4	4.6	7.5	15.7
Hotels, inns, tourist centers (1,170)	518,756	60.0	7.4	.6	1.1	27.8	815.5	151.3	176.1	8.7	74.3	164.5	8.9	2.7	6.9	5.0	15.4
Wine, brandy mfg. (28)	850,000	36.6	5.2	.5	1.6	92.8	68.9	137.6	56.9	49.6	1.6	112.4	3.2	9.1	6.4	8.4	14.9
Women's and misses dresses mfg. (393)	1,500,000	27.9	3.4	1.0	1.8	97.8	145.6	105.8	14.6	40.1	10.5	28.4	9.7	5.4	2.5	5.6	14.5
Stationery stores (931)	402,257	34.6	4.3	1.1	2.7	51.0	71.5	78.9	29.5	30.2	6.6	37.3	5.6	4.9	3.7	7.4	14.1
Book publishing (250)	568,948	42.0	7.1	1.2	2.4	48.5	108.7	67.9	29.6	48.9	5.1	71.5	3.7	5.7	6.9	6.1	13.3
Wood household furnishings mfg. (279)	675,256	29.4	4.8	1.0	2.1	45.1	104.3	76.2	57.9	27.0	9.6	39.7	7.9	4.1	4.1	7.0	13.2
Leather goods mfg. (66)	309,516	31.9	5.4	.8	2.5	42.9	83.1	65.1	35.5	32.8	6.2	52.7	5.2	4.3	5.2	8.1	13.1
Retail nurseries, garden stores (1,089)	340,775	32.0	3.6	.5	1.8	50.9	79.4	78.4	53.2	9.1	5.2	45.1	7.1	4.5	3.2	5.7	12.9
Pottery mfg. (41)	215,798	48.4	11.6	.7	1.5	23.2	66.1	48.7	45.3	29.2	5.6	51.5	3.7	2.6	1.8	5.7	9.9
Doll mfg. (39)	160,000	27.6	2.2	.8	2.0	77.9	94.1	83.1	25.4	48.3	6.7	46.2	6.1	5.2	3.7	3.5	6.0
Membership sports/recreation (744)	569,000	52.9	4.1	1.1	1.6	19.8	635.4	52.0	110.2	38.3	38.0	149.0	7.5	5.1	4.1	2.6	4.5

Source: Industry Norms and Key Business Ratios (Library Edition), Dun & Bradstreet, New York, 1983.

within a business is determined. Again, the ratios regarded as acceptable vary with the type of business, with such factors as seasonality and the basic nature of the business playing major roles. Careful investigation of this key ratio could uncover obsolete inventories or inventories inadequate to the sales requirements of the business.

3. Dividing total assets by total sales provides a gauge of a company's degree of aggressiveness as compared to other companies in its industry. Too low a ratio would indicate insufficient assets for the operation, while too high a ratio would indicate a very conservative operation.
4. Dividing sales by net working capital (net working capital is current assets minus current liability) makes it possible to examine shortages or excesses in liquid funds as related to immediate business requirements. Here a shortage can be an indication of weakness, and an excess, particularly in times of high interest rates, indicates bad business judgment.
5. Dividing accounts payable by annual net sales provides an indication of the extent to which a company uses its suppliers to finance operations. A particularly high ratio would be of concern to short-term creditors.
6. Inventory turn is determined by dividing the cost of goods sold by the average inventory. This ratio provides a measure of how well the inventory dollars are working for the company and, indeed, how good the inventory is. The ratios considered appropriate vary tremendously by industry.

The three profitability ratios must be compared to the goals and aims of management and/or to the alternative uses of money.

1. Return on sales is calculated by dividing net profit after taxes by sales.
2. Return on assets is net profit after taxes divided by total assets and is a measure of the efficiency with which assets are being used.
3. Return on net worth (or equity) is obtained by dividing net profit after taxes by net worth and is the final measure of profitability. However, as is true of all the profitability measurements, in analyzing this ratio, management objectives with regard to salaries and expenses must be examined before any conclusions are reached, as tax and personal considerations frequently play a key role in the formulation of these objectives.

Selected median operating ratios are shown in Table 5–1 on pages 66–67.

MANAGEMENT ACCOUNTING

Management accounting information differs from financial accounting information in that it is neither required by external authorities nor does it have a definitely specified form. Because the information involved in management accounting is generated at the will of the manager, it may cover innumerable situations in unique and individual ways.[6]

For the new business, the ongoing business considering a new direction, or the continuing business undergoing reexamination, there are five general areas of management accounting that deserve attention:

1. The start-up plan.
2. Cash budgeting.
3. Costing.
4. Break-even analysis.
5. The planning budget.

The start-up plan

The start-up plan is simply a method of collecting all of the costs necessary for a new business or a new project in an existing business. The start-up plan shown in Figure 5–2 is typical (see pages 70–71). The estimates stated in column 3 are optimum, and an individual enterprise would tailor this chart to its particular needs and abilities.

The object of the start-up plan is to collect basic information. In order to keep the capitalization requirements at a minimum, it is necessary to put the information of the start-up plan into a time framework, a picture of how the cash will flow in and out of the enterprise over a particular period of time.

Because all new ventures operate on what is referred to as an S curve (a picture of early losses, shown below), the idea of cash flow or cash budgeting is particularly important.

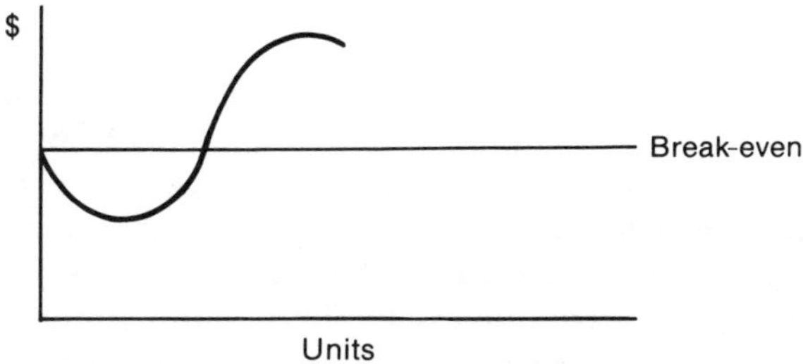

[6]With the penetration of beautifully designed computer software into the accounting sphere, it is reasonable to assume that new standardized techniques for planning, controlling, and coordinating business functions will continue to appear.

FIGURE 5–2 The optimum start-up plan

Estimated monthly expenses

	Your estimate of monthly expenses based on sales of $________	Your estimate of how much cash you need to start your business (see column 3)	What to put in column 2. (These figures are typical for one kind of business. You will have to decide how many months to allow for in your business.)
	Column 1	**Column 2**	**Column 3**
Salary of owner-manager	$	$	2 × column 1
All other salaries and wages			3 × column 1
Rent			3 × column 1
Advertising			3 × column 1
Delivery expense			3 × column 1
Supplies			3 × column 1
Telephone and telegraph			3 × column 1
Other utilities			3 × column 1
Insurance			Payment required by insurance company
Taxes, including social security			4 × column 1
Interest			3 × column 1
Maintenance			3 × column 1
Legal and other professional fees			3 × column 1
Miscellaneous			3 × column 1

Cash flow analysis

Cash flow analysis differs from the income or profit and loss statement in that its basic concern is with the actual inflow and outgo of cash dollars. It has nothing to do with profits except as they are converted into cash. Further, in contrast to the income statement, it treats all cash expenditures in the same way, regardless of whether they eventually become expenses or assets. This is an extremely important distinction for the small businessman, particularly the new venturer. As the S indicates, profits are not the crucial short-range consideration

FIGURE 5–2 ***(concluded)***

	Column 1	Column 2	Column 3
Starting costs you only have to pay once	$	$	Leave column 2 blank
Fixtures and equipment			Fill in worksheet 3 on page 12, and put total here
Decorating and remodeling			Talk it over with a contractor
Installation of fixtures and equipment			Talk to suppliers from whom you buy these
Starting inventory			Suppliers will probably help you estimate this
Deposits with public utilities and landlord			Find out from utilities company and landlord
Legal and other professional fees			Layer, accountant, and so on
Licenses and permits			Find out from city offices what you have to have
Advertising and promotion for opening			Estimate what you'll use
Accounts receivable			What you need to buy more stock until credit customers pay
Cash			For unexpected expenses or losses, special purchases, etc.
Other			Make a separate list and enter total
Total estimated cash you need to start with		$	Add up all the numbers in column 2

TABLE 5–2 Cash flow budget analysis

	January	February	March	April	May	June	July
Projected sales	$20,000	$24,000	$30,000	$24,000	$40,000	$50,000	
Desirable cash balance	5,000	5,000	5,000	5,000	5,000	5,000	$5,00
Receipts:							
Cash (1)	10,000	12,000	15,000	12,000	20,000	25,000	
Expected collection from accounts receivable (2)	—	5,000	11,000	13,500	13,500	16,000	
Total	10,000	17,000	26,000	25,500	33,500	41,000	
Outgo:							
Cash expenses (3)	4,000	4,000	4,000	4,000	4,000	4,000	
Expected accounts payable—merchandise (4)	10,000	12,000	15,000	12,000	20,000	25,000	
Expected accounts payable—start-up (advertising, fixtures, etc.) (5)	20,000	10,000	5,000	—	—	—	
Total	34,000	26,000	24,000	16,000	24,000	29,000	
Difference	(24,000)	(9,000)	2,000	9,500	9,500	12,000	
Desired cash balance (6)	5,000	5,000	5,000	5,000	5,000	5,000	
Amount to be borrowed (7)	29,000	9,000	—	—			
Repayment			2,000	9,500	9,500	12,000	
Loan balance	$29,000	$38,000	$36,000	$26,500	$17,000	$ 5,000	

of the new business. What allows this business to go forward is the cash flow. Income or profits that go into equipment purchases, inventory, or accounts receivable buildups may be irrelevant to profits, but they are potentially crucial as cash drains.

Table 5–2 above is a simplified version of the cash flow chart. For this example, it is assumed (1) that one half of all sales will be for cash and (2) that half of the balance of the invoiced sales will be paid in the next month and half in the following month. It is further assumed (3) that the expense structure of the company (rent, salaries, etc.) is staffed minimally at a $4,000 monthly level and (4) that the inventory can be purchased the month before it is to be sold and must be paid for the following month, the month in which it is sold. Further, (5) start-up expenses totaling $35,000, incurred before the business started, will be paid off in the first three months of operations. Management has also decided (6) that a $5,000 cash balance at the beginning of the month is desirable as a hedge against contingencies. The company has provided for a credit line from a lending source (7) in anticipation of its initial cash flow deficit, with a plan to repay the loan in the first seven months of operations (8).

Costing

We have discussed pricing as an aspect of marketing strategy. We pick the subject up again here in relation to costs, with the understanding that the reader recognizes that costs are an element in pricing, but not the determining element. Only the market and the marketing strategy can set price. Costs, however arrived at, are a way of evaluating the company's competitive position, a way of testing its assumptions and its competitive efficiency in implementing those assumptions.

Business costs are a combination of fixed and variable expenses. Fixed costs include all the expenses that exist regardless of whether you produce anything. In the simplest kind of analysis, such things as heat, light, and rent, as well as any other ongoing expenses that the manager considers untouchable in the short run, are considered fixed costs.

Variable costs are those expenses that increase only as the product or service is provided and include the costs of direct labor and materials. Variable costs relate most directly to the cost of goods sold figure of the income statement. In the simplified version of the business enterprise shown in Table 5–2, the $4,000 monthly operating expense was considered fixed. It is the cost of doing business.[7] The merchandise being sold cost 50 percent of the ultimate selling price, a dollar amount variable with volume.

In planning a business project, the manager should thoroughly understand these relationships because they involve everything from short-range jeopardy to the possibility of high long-range profits. For example, the greater the ratio of fixed costs to variable costs, the more severe the low-volume risks and the greater the possibility of high-volume profit. At the same time, it is important to realize that the higher the fixed (or entry) costs, the more difficult it is for competition to develop. When evaluating fixed costs such as rent or major machinery, this is a major consideration. On the other hand, a business that can achieve its desired unique quality through variations on the product costs—packaging and similar costs that vary only with volume—minimizes risk because such costs are incurred only as sales are consummated. We have already discussed this concept in relation to the cost of sales personnel. If a salesperson is paid a salary, he represents a

[7] We have omitted references to profit in this costing process because it is our assumption that profit—or capital available for future investment—is best considered in the same way as any other cost.

fixed cost. If he is paid a commission on his sales, he represents a variable cost because he is paid only for what he sells. If he receives a salary plus commission, part of his compensation is a fixed cost, part a variable cost.

When expenditures can be separated in this way, a method of costing a product or service evolves, provided that it is possible to estimate sales volume, the number of units that can be sold at a given price. When sales volume can be estimated, the manager can divide the costs of doing business (or overhead costs) by the number of units he can sell at a given price and thus determine the dollar amount of overhead, or fixed costs, that must be allocated to each unit.

$$\frac{\text{Dollar cost of doing business}}{\text{Anticipated unit sales}} = \begin{array}{c}\text{Dollar cost of doing}\\ \text{business allocated}\\ \text{to each unit}\end{array}$$

If the manager already knows his variable cost percentage, by totaling the two he can arrive at his per unit cost. This formula is most easily applied when the selling price is set by analysis of market competition. Costs determined in this way indicate to the businessperson whether or not his cost structure is competitive.

A similar process is involved in service businesses where the elements normally involved in the costs of goods sold are either not significant or not easily identified. In such cases, virtually all of the costs of the business become costs of doing business, overhead costs. Here the enterprise is selling what it costs to be in business for a specific period of time—the time necessary to perform a particular task—and therefore the overhead costs must be divided by hours to determine a "billable" price per project hour.[8]

$$\frac{\text{Cost of doing business per period}}{\text{Hours available per period}} = \text{Billable cost}$$

Break-even analysis

The crucial problem of the various costing formulas is the sales projection. The technique that deals with this most difficult aspect of being in business is known as break-even analysis. Break-even analysis takes the figures that are known and provides answers to the question "What if?"

Figure 5–3 provides a graphic presentation of the cost picture shown in Table 5–2. The presentation assumes that the selling price of each unit is $100.

[8]This is an oversimplification because it assumes that all available hours can be assigned to specific projects. When this is not the case, a relationship between hours available and project hours must be determined.

FIGURE 5–3 Break-even analysis

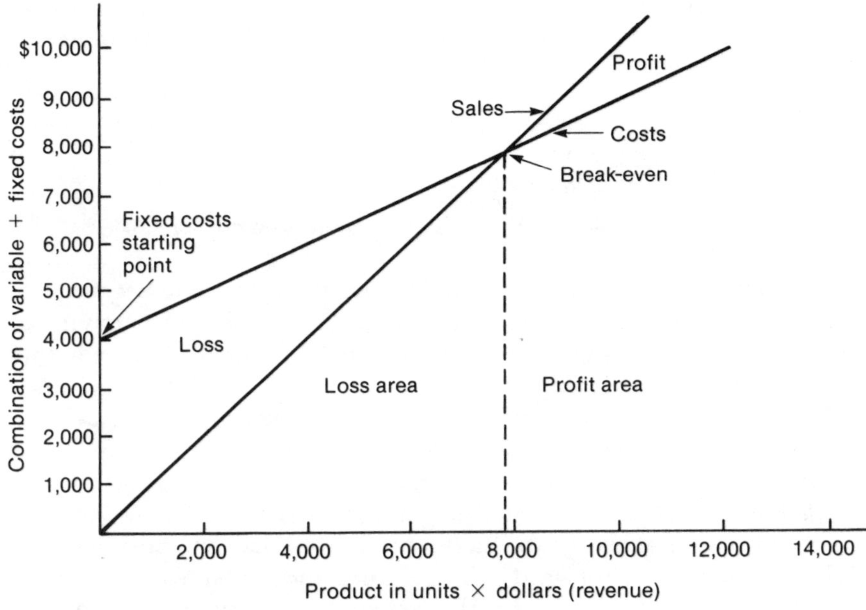

Units	20	40	60	80	100
Fixed costs	$4,000	$4,000	$4,000	$4,000	$ 4,000
Variable costs at 50 percent of selling price	1,000	2,000	3,000	4,000	5,000
	5,000	6,000	7,000	8,000	9,000
Sales at $100 each	2,000	4,000	6,000	8,000	10,000
Profit (loss)	(3,000)	(2,000)	(1,000)	—	1,000

Another way to look at this is to take the difference between the actual (variable) cost of the product in terms of labor and materials and the proposed selling price; determine the gross margin, or contribution to overhead; and divide that into your fixed cost to determine how many units you have to sell to break even:

$100	Selling price
50	Cost
$ 50	Gross profit (per unit dollar contribution to fixed costs)

$4,000 (fixed costs) ÷ $50 (per unit contribution) = 80 units to break even

This may be done by using the actual dollar gross profit that produces the unit figure necessary for break even or by using the gross profit figure as a percentage of sales (50 percent) that will produce the dollar revenue necessary to break even:

$100	Selling price
50	Cost
$ 50	Gross profit (50 percent of selling price)

$4,000 ÷ $50 = 80 units to break even

As we have said, break-even analysis provides the clue necessary to anticipate volume by supplying a number to consider. On arriving at this number, the businessman must make a judgment as to whether that sales level is realistic.

We have consistently pointed out in our marketing chapters that it is essential to differentiate the product or service in some way, to develop the appeals, the value satisfactions, that give life and viability to the enterprise. Break-even analysis makes clear that the cost of each differentiating element of the value satisfaction package must be justifiable in the straightforward terms of sales and dollar volume. Let us see how by returning to our break-even analysis. Assume that management decides that a $1,000 monthly advertising program is necessary to differentiate its product. Fixed costs then rise to $5,000 a month. Management then has two choices: (1) it can decide that the advertising will increase sales by 20 units, that real volume will increase and thus justify the decision; or (2) it can decide to raise its selling price by $12.50 (the additional cost divided by the old number of units) and thus recover the new cost on the old volume. The latter choice is technically referred to as raising the gross margin or gross profit.

We stated early in this book that profit was not the purpose of a business enterprise but the test of its validity. By this, we meant that a business enterprise can be successful only if its assumptions about the market are valid. A company's ability to create customers is the measure of its success. If a company's assumptions about how the market will respond to its value satisfaction package are wrong, if the results of those assumptions do not justify their costs, then proof exists that the assumptions are not valid and should therefore be changed. The technique of break-even analysis illustrates this thesis.

The planning budget

The planning budget, the final management accounting device that we will consider here, is an offshoot of the income statement. Its principal use is to relate periodic progress to year-end goals. It is a cross between the income statement and the cash budget in that it measures the progress of the business during the accounting period *according to where the business is projected to be.* Like other tools of management accounting, it is intended to be used internally.

The essential element of the planning budget is the estimate of profit or loss for periods shorter than a year. The value of the planning budget is most obvious in highly seasonal businesses whose actual profits are realized in a few months. The measure of performance that must be noted is how close the business comes to its predicted course; the analysis determines where the variances occurred.

Using a simplified illustration, a projected (pro forma) income statement for a year (January 1 to December 31) might show:

Sales	$100,000	100	(percent)
Cost of goods sold	40,000	40	
Gross margin	60,000	60	
Expenses	40,000	40	
Net profit before taxes	20,000	20	

The question that the businessperson wants answered is, "How am I doing at the end of March?" Because it would be unrealistic to expect 25 percent of his profit to have been earned at that time, he can obtain the answer to this question only if he has broken down his expectations by quarters. As with other management accounting devices, the methodology of the planning budget can be self-determined. For example, an expense item that is purchased once a year can be spread out over 12 months or considered in the month it is received. The key is to relate actual performance to expectation and to discover variances when they occur so that they may be corrected. The tendency to "hope" that things will improve can be overcome through the judicious use of the planning budget.

SUGGESTED READINGS

Anthony, Robert N., and James S. Reese. *Accounting Principles.* 4th ed. Homewood, Ill: Richard D. Irwin, 1979.

Aragon, George A. *A Manager's Complete Guide to Financial Techniques.* New York: Free Press, 1982.

6 The sources of funding

The subject of financing (like the numbers discussed in the previous chapter) is often needlessly intimidating to the small businessman. Because the world of money is a world with its own language, its own rules, and its own inhabitants, the small businessman frequently views that world as he would any other foreign entity, either from a safe distance or with great trepidation.

Failure to deal with the financial structure of a new or ongoing business in forthright, realistic, and enlightened terms is a mistake that inevitably forces business managers to make bad decisions. Inadequate cash flow leads to poor operating practices, such as not taking trade discounts, and frequently forces the small businessman to make improper strategic choices with regard to location, purchasing, hiring, and sales promotion.[1]

The pressures that come from working with inadequate funding are not necessarily a part of being in business, and therefore it is incum-

---

[1]To determine how much not taking a trade discount costs, utilize this formula:

$$\frac{\text{Discount}}{100 - \text{Discount}} \times \frac{360}{\text{Payment period} - \text{Discount period}}$$

Assume that the purchase terms allow a 2 percent discount if payment is made within 10 days of invoicing. If payment is not made within 10 days, the customer has a total of 30 days in which to pay, receiving no discount.

$$\frac{2}{100 - 2} \times \frac{360}{30 - 10} = 36.7\%$$

on an annualized basis, assuming that this is a continual practice.

bent upon the serious manager to explore his financial resources fully before embarking on a new venture or redirecting the course of an ongoing venture.

As discussed in Chapter 4, the financial structure of a business is divided into the equity, or the ownership share, and the debt, the amount that is borrowed. In this chapter, we will concentrate on debt financing, deferring the consideration of the primary capital structure to Chapter 8 with just one exception. The person who is considering a new business should acknowledge the fact that the right to borrow is not constitutionally guaranteed—it must be earned. While there are noteworthy exceptions (smaller banks, for example), many prospective lenders insist on a track record—a number of years in business, a specified minimum sales volume, etc.—before they will consider a loan. Thus, the potential small businessman should also look to his personal assets (including cash surrender value of his life insurance, personal credit card lines, real estate equity, etc.) in considering the proposed financial structure of his new venture. The question "Would I lend money to this applicant?" is a useful guideline.

CRITERIA FOR THE SELECTION OF FUNDING SOURCES

There are a great number of ways to supplement the equity of a business venture. The key to the selection of the most appropriate method is to match the goals and character of the enterprise with those of the prospective funding source. To do this, one must determine the character of the venture (is it a wild idea or a conventional idea, a high-risk situation or a low-risk situation, international or local, etc.), determine which of the possible funding sources are similar in character, and communicate that similarity to those funding sources, thereby convincing them that the proposed investment is well thought out, viable, and appropriate to their specific objectives. The goal is to obtain a proper "fit" between the venture and its funding source.

The borrowing equation must balance the degree of risk on one side against the potential for gain on the other. All of the sources engaged in the commercial supply of money are seeking methods of utilizing their funds. Money, broadly speaking, is their inventory, what they have to sell. Unless they move that inventory, they cannot make a profit. The amount that these sources charge and their choice of means of payment depend on their evaluation of the risk in relation to the prospective return. The "price" they attach to the risk factor may vary from simple interest to an equity position in the company, depending on the source.

The key point that the prospective borrower must recognize is that the different financial sources have different "business" objectives, ranging from the public policy objectives of government agencies to the more easily understood objective of profit maximization. The situations under which these sources will offer funds must be consistent with their objectives. The small businessman can go a long way toward eliminating his apprehensions in the area of financing if, in investigating possible lending sources, he bears in mind the fact that what motivates them is the satisfaction of their individual objectives. Frequently these sources are in business in the same way as the potential recipient of their funds is in business: the bank branch manager is judged on his ability to bring in new business; the fund manager must invest to survive; the SBIC must leverage its loan. On the other hand, the father-in-law who is willing to sign a personal bank note to finance his son-in-law's business has a vastly different goal. Each case, each source, must be considered separately.

Timing deserves the same consideration here as it receives in other buyer-seller relationships. For example, fluctuations in interest rates and other factors affect the amount of money that a bank can lend, and its lending standards may vary with such fluctuations.

Because each potential financial source evaluates the probability of success for the business venture in its own terms, the prospective borrower must recognize and understand those terms before approaching a prospective source of funds. The difference between the point of view of the venture capitalist seeking an outlet for "seed" capital and that of the commercial bank attempting to sell short-term money is enormous, and that difference is crucial to the prospective borrower.

FUNDING AND THE CREDIBILITY OF THE BORROWER

No matter what the borrower's request, the major element in his negotiation package is "credibility." What convinces a potential source of funds that a concept and a set of projections are believable, and therefore creditworthy, varies from situation to situation, but among the major factors that make for "credibility" are the following:

1. Previous experience. The ideal situation is one in which the applicant for a loan has recently succeeded in doing exactly the same thing that he now proposes to do.
2. Introduction by a respected professional—a lawyer, an accountant, or a business broker, for example—who is a current client of the lender. The achievement of reliability by association, particularly with respected members of the accounting and legal professions, is common in business. (Assuming that one will require the

services of an accountant and a lawyer, seeking a recommendation from the potential lending source is often a good move as well as a reverse means of achieving reliability by association.)

3. The thoroughness of the business plan and projection, including a comfortable program for the amount, timing, and repayment schedule of the loan.
4. The appropriateness of the choice of the lender and the consistency in the point of view of the application. For example, a major factor in the selection of a proposed lender would be the importance that the proposed lender attaches to the debt-equity ratio discussed in the previous chapter. Commercial banks place great stress on such ratios and use them both to compare businesses with one another and as measures of the health of a particular business. For other types of lenders, such ratios may not be a pertinent consideration. Where capital growth, for example, is the primary concern of the lender, the evaluation of the market and the proposed strategy would be more central to the lender's interest.

RISK AND THE COSTS OF FUNDING

Among most money suppliers, the general rule is that the higher the risk to the lender, the more the borrower has to give to get the money. If we start with the assumption that the potential money supplier has the option of placing its available funds in various nonrisk situations—banks, government securities, bonds of various types, and so on—it is obvious that a premium must be attached to placing those funds with a specific business enterprise. That premium may take many forms. In banks, where the interest charged is the cost of the money, the theoretical benchmark is called the "prime rate," the interest rate that the bank supposedly charges its most desirable customers. Depending on the risk, the rate charged a particular lender will rise or fall (within certain upward limits) above or below this rate.

What the business enterprise is willing to pay for the funds it borrows depends on its short- and long-run needs. What the business enterprise has to give in return for the funds it borrows is money (to be derived or "borrowed" from future income), control (either voting or limited veto power), a favored position with regard to supply, or participation in the current or future potential of the business, that is, an equity position or a privileged future position. Arrangements based on one or more of these concessions can be simple or extremely sophisticated, but these are the general possibilities.

There are basically three types of lenders—no-risk lenders, calculated-risk lenders, and high-risk lenders. No-risk lenders are primarily banks; calculated-risk lenders are commercial finance companies; and high-risk lenders are by definition some form of venture capitalists. In each situation, the degree of risk that lenders assume must be met by a compensating degree of return, ranging from simple investment to equity. Personal and private sources may fall anywhere in this spectrum. (Lenders in this case are not to be confused with the nonactive contributors toward the initial capitalization, who may be either stockholders or limited partners.)

Simple borrowing from either a bank or a private source is perhaps the most common source of nonequity business funds. Practically speaking, in the case of a low-risk lender the availability of funds depends on the lender's perception of the borrower's ability to repay within a specified period of time and the lender's perception of the degree to which its risk is protected. All funding resources consider the degree of the borrower's experience in the contemplated business the major judgmental factor in this regard.

Generally speaking, the banker's income is dependent, not on the profitability of the client company, but on his own ability to produce safe, trouble-free business. Thus the banker's investigation of marketing strategy, pro forma profit and loss projections, and cash flow analysis is aimed, not at determining how much money the company might make, but at verifying the feasibility of the payback schedule. To further ensure the safety of the investment, the banker is interested in the security offered by the borrower. This security usually involves the assets of the business—the owners' equity, either in cash or other forms; patents; accounts receivable; or physical assets such as equipment, inventory, and plant. Personal guarantees are also major considerations here, whether or not the business is incorporated.

As we have noted, banks depend much more heavily on the financial ratios discussed in the previous chapter than do other types of lending institutions. Most banks limit themselves to short-term loans except when specific assets are pledged.

The degree of business counseling available from a lender could be a major factor in the borrower's choice. That degree can vary tremendously even within the same category of lender. The lending sources interested in riskier ventures are inclined to provide direct management assistance, through participation on boards of directors or less formal means. Such assistance is often an indication of their preoccupation with the marketing idea rather than the management. Smaller banks tend to deal with smaller businesses, and banks with a particular expertise tend to prefer to exercise that expertise. (Here the primary thrust of the business can be the basis for guidelines in the selection of a lender. If the business is related to a particular trade, for example, a bank with experience in that trade is more likely to be helpful; if location is a key factor in the business operation, a bank in the geographic area involved is more likely to relate to specific assumptions; etc.)

FUNDING BY CREDITORS

A less expensive form of financing, but one that is often overlooked, has to do with the extended payment terms allowed by potential creditors. Frequently payment terms for some start-up costs—equipment, supplies, inventory—can be stretched out, depending on the self-interest of the supplier. A decision to seek significant funds or credit from such a supplier should be viewed as if the supplier were any other source of funds, and the approach should be as thoughtful. Projections, strategies, and the like are of interest to many prospective suppliers.

A similar opportunity exists among potential product or service buyers. Such buyers may perceive an investment in the company to be in their self-interest, particularly when it offers a unique product or service, and thus may provide funds—either cash or short payment terms—as well as a ready market.

Conventional trade credit is a major source of nonequity funding—one that the small businessman should be very familiar with because he himself will frequently be a grantor as well as a recipient of such credit. Trade credit is often a result of an evaluation by a major credit agency such as Dun & Bradstreet that makes information available to its subscribers with recommendations as to credit maximums. A D&B rating (evaluation) is available to subscribers either in periodically published industry books or through reports supplied by the agency after investigation by its field reporters. A firm may obtain such a rating by submitting financial statements to the agency's representatives.

The D&B "capital and credit" rating consists of two parts: estimated financial strength and a composite credit appraisal (see Table 6–1). The estimated financial strength factor is directly related to net worth or equity, and the composite appraisal is a number derived from an analysis of four major items that have historically proven to be major factors in the success or failure of a business.

The general principles employed by D&B are similar to those used by other such agencies and provide excellent guidelines for judging any business. Credit granted under these guidelines is appropriate to the estimated strength of the company.

THE SALE OF TAX SHELTERS

The other side of the trade credit coin—quick payment by purchasers—may also be a source of funds for the astute manager. Induc-

TABLE 6–1 Dun & Bradstreet ratings

A typical Dun & Bradstreet credit rating is made up of two parts, estimated fina cial strength and a composite credit appraisal. The rating is a letter/number combin tion, such as BB1. The letter and number equivalents are based on the following cha Estimated financial worth is essentially the equity figure—capital plus retained ear ings or total assets minus total liabilities. The composite credit appraisal is explain below. Ratings of 1R (net worth in excess of $125,000) or 2R (net worth in excess $50,000) are used when actual book figures are not available and reliable estimates c be found. D&B maintains slightly different systems for different industries, but th are all variations of this chart.

Factors considered in composite credit appraisal ratings (1, 2, 3, 4)

	1st line (high)	2d line (good)	3d line (fair)	4th line (limited
	If all conditions listed below are favorable	If most conditions listed below are favorable	Still considered creditworthy, but with some of the following unfavorable elements	Even greater elements of risk creditworthines limited
Payments	Satisfactory, suitable explanations for any slownesses	Generally satisfactory, suitable explanations for slownesses	Significant slownesses	Significant, even chronic, slownesses
Finance	Statements regularly obtained Usually comparative figures Strong condition Upward trend	Statement obtained Sound condition Trend usually favorable	Statement obtained Condition unbalanced Operating losses Impaired cash flow Heavy debt	Statement obtain Condition unbalanced Even heavier loss and debt
History	One year old, at least; three years preferably Adequate assurance of ownership	No minimum years if other factors satisfactory Adequate assurance of ownership	Adequate assurance of ownership	Adequate assuran of ownership
Antecedents	Experienced in all aspects of business management No recent business failures, felony convictions, etc., that would have serious impact on business	If new, previous experience in line or in successfully managing a previous business No recent business failures, felony convictions, etc., that would have serious impact on business	May lack balanced experience or experience in line Consider impact on business of failures or felony convictions	May lack balance experience or experience in li Consider impact business of any recent business failures or felo convictions
Other	Other factors to be considered for their possible favorable or unfavorable influence o a business include operation or location, bank record, public record information, general economic factors, industry, or local conditions.			

TABLE 6–1 ***(concluded)***

Key to ratings

Estimated financial strength		High	Good	Fair	Limited
		Composite credit appraisal			
5A	$50 million and over	1	2	3	4
4A	$10,000,000 to 49,999,999	1	2	3	4
3A	1,000,000 to 9,999,999	1	2	3	4
1A	750,000 to 999,999	1	2	3	4
BA	500,000 to 749,999	1	2	3	4
BB	200,000 to 499,999	1	2	3	4
CB	125,000 to 199,999	1	2	3	4
CC	75,000 to 124,999	1	2	3	4
DC	50,000 to 74,999	1	2	3	4
DD	35,000 to 49,999	1	2	3	4
EE	20,000 to 34,999	1	2	3	4
FF	10,000 to 19,999	1	2	3	4
GG	5,000 to 9,999	1	2	3	4
HH	Up to $4,999	1	2	3	4

ing a customer to pay in advance may be very desirable. This is often done by means of special incentive payment terms, allowing a discount for early payment. Since this funding method can be expensive, it must be examined carefully and compared to the current cost and availability of other funding methods.

A modification of this nonequity method of financing that is very much in vogue at the moment is the sale of certain tax shelter provisions. While this is a highly technical subject that generally requires the counsel of professionals, the basic approach stems from government policies that have been incorporated into the tax code. In its desire to encourage such things as the increased productivity of natural and physical resources and business innovation, the government has allowed such business costs as exploration, research and development, and equipment purchases to be deducted by a business from income taxes due in the year that those costs are incurred. Business start-up costs, such as the building of subscription lists, may also be deducted as a business expense in the year that the items are developed instead of being spread out over the time that the company uses them. As we have pointed out in the S curve illustration, the business usually shows a loss in its early life, and such special expenses can make that loss significant.

In the case of tax shelters, the business in effect sells its loss to someone who can deduct it from his income and thus effect a cash savings on his income tax payments. Tax shelters are attractive to high-income investors who are interested in short-term tax reduction.

The simple method through which tax shelters are obtained is the limited partnership agreement. While the tax shelter provisions provide an attractive short-range method of attracting loans or investments, the business that obtains funds in this way deprives itself of a legitimate tax advantage that can be carried forward into its first growth years. The normal tax shelter package involves a cash inflow for a business in its early years, for which it may give up some profit participation later on. There is normally a maximum term of 10 to 15 years on such arrangements. While tax shelters seem to be a good method of acquiring additional funds, they are difficult and expensive to set up, and they are coming under closer scrutiny by tax officials.

FACTORING AND FINANCING

Commercial finance companies have essentially the same point of view as banks, with one major exception. Their primary concern is self-protection. They lack the feeling of benevolent paternalism that often characterizes banks. They are willing to become involved in higher-risk situations for larger fees. Typically, such involvement comes in the accounts receivable area, where they will offer financing based on sales and invoicing as they occur. Their procedures and rates vary according to their perception of risk. They may take over complete responsibility for accounts receivable (factoring), or they may loan money against your collection (financing). The charges of commercial finance companies are normally based on a fee (percentage) for the loan and an amount for the service provided.

The acceptance of various national credit cards (American Express, MasterCard, etc.) by retail establishments is similar in concept to factoring and thus eliminates the accounts receivable cash requirement.

VENTURE CAPITAL FUNDS

Corresponding with the interest in entrepreneurship in recent years has been the rise in venture capital funds. While no more than 10 such funds existed in 1970, the current number probably exceeds 250.

Although the objectives and methods of venture capital funds vary greatly, their general approach is to exchange an equity interest for a financial (and often management) participation in the early years of a company's development. They hold the equity interest only until they can sell it at a substantial profit. The multiples for such funds depend on their perception of the risk and how long they expect to have their investment tied up. On the high-risk side, the multiples may be 10 times the investment in 5 years or 4 times the investment in 3 years; on the low-risk side, they may be 7 times the investment in 10 years and 3 times the investment in 3 years.[2]

Venture capital funds are of most interest to high-technology companies or other companies with very strong potential for rapid growth. The strength of venture capital funds in the funding market has been growing significantly because of the recent reduction in the maximum capital gains rate and the visible success of a number of venture capital firms.

The formula commonly used in the venture capital field is $V = P \times S \times M$, where V = Value, P = Problem, S = Solution, and M = Management. (The terms *problem* and *solution* as used here have the same meaning as the needs and means of satisfaction discussed in earlier chapters.) Because venture capitalists are primarily interested in the kind of return on investment that comes from high growth where substantial dollars are concerned, their focus is on the problem that the prospective company is attempting to solve. The greater the problem (disease, hunger, aging, etc.), the greater are the possibilities of return and the greater is the degree of interest of the venture capitalist.

The solution that the prospective client offers to that problem is the second consideration of the venture capitalist. The better the solution, the greater are the chances of success.

Finally, and this is the point of greatest difference between the venture capitalist and the traditional lending sources, the venture capitalist evaluates the management of a company and its ability to implement the solution to the problem only after he has accepted the problem and solution as worthwhile. Because the venture capital fund frequently demands a participation in management for the term of its financial relationships with a company, it views its own management ability (and its ability to obtain additional outside help) as a part of its contribution. The feeling of the typical venture capitalist is that if the problem is great and the solution is acceptable, the management effort can be buttressed. If neither the problem nor the solution meets the growth potential requirement of the venture capitalist, the skill of management is generally considered to be irrelevant.

The best venture capital funds can make an enormous contribution to the fledgling entrepreneur because their great experience with start-up companies has given them unusual expertise in the risks and pitfalls of the early phases. Of course, the high-risk participant is not limited to the formal venture capital funds but may include any investor who is seeking a high return on capital investment.

---

[2]In other words, in the first illustration above, if the venture capitalist feels that his money will be tied up for five years, he will finance the investment if he can increase the capital he commits by 10 times in that period.

Variations on the venture capital funds include corporations that enter into lending or partial equity financing, not in order to achieve capital gains income, but for such purposes as positioning themselves in new technologies or utilizing excess or unknown plant or product capacity. This area of financing is of growing interest to major corporations.

A further variation of higher-risk financing may be found in either the SBIC (Small Business Investment Company) or the MESBIC (Minority Enterprise Small Business Investment Company).

These companies had their beginning after World War II, when the government was persuaded to fund a "development bank" to aid small businesses. This device supplied low-cost loans to private investment corporations at a ratio of $4 in loan money to $1 in equity capital, with direct guidelines as to the size of the companies that would be eligible for financing help from the newly formed SBIC. This idea was supplemented in the late 60s, when the Office of Minority Business Enterprises developed a similar plan called the Minority Enterprise Small Business Investment Company, primarily to assist blacks in doing business in the inner city. This plan was amended in 1976 with a broader definition of "minorities."

In practice, the principal difference between the various SBICs and the private venture capital funds involves the objectives of the participant. The private venture capitalists are looking for shorter-term investments with more substantial capital gains. The SBICs are required by charter to look for longer-term investments (full repayment is not allowed within five years) and a steady return on the investment. Typically, the SBIC requires substantial interest payment during the early years of investment, which the private venture capitalists will forgo, and takes a much tougher position on risk protection. While the private venture capitalist generally seeks businesses with a very rapid growth potential, the usual SBIC is aimed at more conventional businesses.

PUBLIC FUNDING

The various business development corporations and their offshoots are another source of public funding. These programs, aimed primarily at manufacturers and other substantial users of low-skilled labor, are run by state and local governments with the intention of creating jobs. Their financing may take the form of plant financing, job training subsidies, tax abatements, and/or general loans.

The formal funding source of last resort is the U.S. Small Business Administration, which was organized and funded by the government in 1953 to help small companies by supplying counsel and money. Because the banks feared unfair competition from the lower interest rates offered by the SBA, the original concept was amended so that applications for direct loans from the SBA can be made only after the applicant has been rejected by at least two banks.

The SBA may also guarantee up to 90 percent of the loans made to qualifying small businesses by banks. The request for such participation must be made by the bank rather than the individual borrower. (To place this matter in perspective, in New York, the largest SBA region, the SBA makes only 10 to 20 direct loans per quarter; 90 percent of the loans granted by the SBA are of the bank guarantee variety.)

While there is flexibility within the SBA setup, it should be noted that the primary applicants are persons toward whom the government has some feeling of ongoing responsibility—veterans, the handicapped, and the economically and socially disadvantaged. Unemployment, conservation, mass transit, such industries as the energy industry, and economic development in depressed areas are also target situations for the SBA. This does not mean, however, that SBA participation is limited to such cases.

The requirements for SBA loans are obviously more flexible than those of the commercial banks. This is particularly apparent in the time limits on repayment and in the acceptable relationship between equity and collateral. Where a bank typically might look for a 2:1 debt-to-equity ratio, the SBA might accept a 4:1 ratio.

A very valuable SBA service is the counseling program offered through SCORE/ACE (Service Corps of Retired Executives and Active Corps of Executives). At the various SBA offices throughout the country, a pool of experts on various types of businesses provides free counseling on all matters relating to small business. This service includes field visits. In addition, seminars and publications on various topics are offered on a continuing basis.

SUGGESTED READINGS

Pratt, Stanley E. *How to Raise Venture Capital.* New York: Charles Scribner's Sons, 1982.

Silver, A. David. *Up Front Financing.* New York: John Wiley & Sons, 1982.

7 Buying a business

As we have indicated, the shortest route to success in small business is the purchase of an existing business.

ADVANTAGES AND DISADVANTAGES

The advantages of purchasing an existing business are clear. Unlike a business that the manager starts from scratch, an existing business provides a set of performance guidelines that may be used as a planning base. Typically, it has a history from which sales and costs can be projected. It usually has people in place who have demonstrated capability at a predictable level. It has an image that can be characterized, a direction that can serve as a point of departure. The time frame in which it operates can be stated with assurance. The S curve problems that we mentioned in Chapter 5 can be bypassed.

The major disadvantages of purchasing an existing business are also clear. You may not be buying what you think. Reliable information is not always available. The existing interpersonal relations may be tenuous. You may be inheriting an irreversible negative pattern. Even if you set aside difficulties ranging from outright deception by the seller to those against which the buyer can protect himself by taking reasonable care, formidable judgment factors are involved in buying what at best is a partially submerged iceberg. And more important, by buying a business that already exists, you may not be getting exactly what you want, the business that is appropriate to your particular needs.

THE STREAM OF INCOME AND ITS CAPITALIZATION

From the buyer's point of view, purchase of an existing business is not so much the purchase of clearly identifiable physical assets (except as downside protection) as the purchase of a "stream of income." The stream of income is a key concept that is often disregarded in approaching this subject because traditionally when we think about buying, we think about buying something tangible.[1] In purchasing a business, the "capitalization" of the stream of income or profit is the course to be pursued because the principal concern of the purchaser must be the future, not the present, not the physical assets as they stand, but the physical assets only as they contribute to the business flow.

On the face of it, the capitalization of earnings seems to be a fairly simple problem. Using audited statements or other verifiable data and assuming that you could view that flow of income over a five-year period (over and above reasonable salaries, etc.) and find that it averages, say, $20,000 a year, it would be relatively easy to determine that the business was worth whatever a similar return would cost elsewhere, in the certificate of deposit market, for example. If the rate of return in the market is 11 percent, and this is the rate of return wanted from the business, the $20,000 annual income would require an investment of $181,818 ($20,000 ÷ .11). But accepting this rate of return would assume that the investment is as safe as investment in the CD market. If, on the other hand, you consider the investment half as safe as investment in the CD market, you might seek double the return on investment offered by that market—22 percent, or ($20,000 ÷ .22), of $90,909.

Let's apply this line of reasoning to the Small Publishing Company (see Table 7–1). Its average income over the past three years was $70,000. Capitalizing that amount at 22 percent, we come to an evaluation of the income stream at $318,181.

The mathematical computations are simple enough. The difficulties revolve around the various assumptions, ranging from the establishment of the capitalization rate to the profit estimates. (Profit estimates may be particularly tricky because the previous owner may have employed unusual expenses and similar devices to avoid income taxes.)

---

[1]We do not mean to imply here that the value of the physical assets is to be ignored—only that it is a secondary rather than a primary consideration. Ratio analysis as outlined in Chapter 5 affords the basic approach to asset evaluation, and it should certainly be used in conjunction with the stream of income technique.

TABLE 7–1

	12/31/82	Percent	12/31/81	Percent	12/31/80	Percent
Net sales	$1,200,000		$900,000		$1,100,000	
Cost of goods sold	840,000	70	648,000	72	803,000	73
Gross profit	360,000	30	252,000	28	297,000	27
Selling, administrative, and general expense	256,000	21.3	232,000	25.7	211,000	19.1
Net profit before taxes	$ 104,000	8.6	$ 20,000	2	$ 86,000	7.8

SMALL PUBLISHING COMPANY
Balance Sheet
December 31, 1982

Assets		Liabilities	
Cash	$ 12,000	Accounts payable	$112,000
Accounts receivable	218,000	Accrued expense	62,000
Inventory	306,000	Taxes payable	24,000
	536,000	Other	198,000
Plant	200,000	Net worth	450,000
Accumulated depreciation	180,000		
	20,000		
Equipment	115,000		
Accumulated depreciation	23,000		
	92,000		
Total assets	$648,000	Total liabilities and net worth	$648,000

THE BUYER'S CONSIDERATIONS

All of the elements of business planning that have been discussed earlier in this book come into play in the establishment of a buy/sell price and agreement. All of the internal and external factors influencing sales and marketing should be investigated as thoroughly as possible. Particular attention should be paid to how the company is regarded by its customers and to the extent of its customer base. The possibility that the market will be affected by new factors—product obsolescence, new competition, changing buying patterns, and so on—must be considered. Industry ratios and demographic and psychographic observations are important as evidence of positive or negative movement. Similarly, the resource structure must be evaluated—is it reliable, steady? If the resource is a particular type of skilled labor, how difficult is it to replace that supply? Is the gross margin under pressure? Are the operating expenses reasonable? Do the salaries and the travel and entertaining expenses make sense? Are there "quirks" to this particular situation, such as an unfortunate dependency on currency fluctuations, zoning changes, or other extra-business factors?[2]

The buyer must also ask, "Is this business of interest to me?" and "How does this business relate to my particular abilities?" What will you contribute to this business over a period of time that will give satisfaction as well as profit? We have pointed out that profit follows if the customer's needs are satisfied. Here we are saying that profit follows if the businessman's needs are satisfied. What do I want to do? What can I do to guarantee that the business reaches its goal? Many prospective businesspeople do not take the breather necessary to answer these questions. Caught up in the enthusiasm of the purchase, they do not take the time needed to evaluate it from a personal perspective. "Is this the way I want to spend my days and nights?" is a question that can be asked here for the last time.

The third major area that the buyer must investigate is what the sale of the business is worth to the seller. Relating the answer to the requirements of the buyer is the key to what has become known as "win-win" negotiation. It is not necessary for one person to win and the other to lose in a negotiation; both sides must come as close to their objectives as possible. For the buyer, it becomes important to understand what the seller's personal and business objectives are, what limits he is willing to impose on those objectives, and what alterna-

[2]The same considerations are examined in Chapter 10 in the discussion of the business plan prepared for submission to a funding source. Thus this chapter and Chapter 10 may be read sequentially.

tives to the sale proposition are available to him. The simplistic answer "It is worth the most he can get" does not take into consideration such matters as the relationship of extended payments to total dollar management (tax considerations, etc.) or the desire for continued participation or the continued employment for family members. A sensitivity to such matters is crucial to the idea of win-win negotiation.

Finally, there is the question of how to finance the purchase. Remembering that a going concern is usually bankable, always consider the best possible combination—the leveraged buyout with management participation. This is a method of using the assets of the company to allow the purchase. It calls for borrowing against the assets and asking the seller for extended terms or similar loans (or loan guarantees) to make up the purchase price.

AN EXAMPLE

The case of the Small Publishing Company is again illustrative.

Assume that the negotiated selling price falls halfway between the book net worth of the company ($450,000) and the figure arrived at by the capitalization of earnings ($318,181), or $384,090. Assume a modest ($34,090) contribution of capital by the new owner. The first question to resolve is whether, if the new owner is fortunate enough to finance the entire balance of the purchase price (for example, $350,000 at 15 percent = $52,500 in interest against a 1982 before-tax profit of $104,000), the cash flow of the business is able to carry the debt-generated outgo. If the answer is no, the prospective purchaser requires additional equity capital. If the answer is yes, he has to look to the assets of the company for assets that may be borrowed against, applying the appropriate ratios in the search for loan opportunities. What is the plant really worth? How good are the accounts receivable? Can the accounts payable be extended? Can the inventory be reduced? What was the owner's salary? What were his expenses? Because the Small Publishing Company has no debt, it is obviously a prime candidate for a leveraged buyout. And while we have used a rather clear-cut illustration to make the point, the method is the message.

The question of the previous owner's participation arises when the prospective purchaser does not wish (or is not able) to pay the $34,090 and $350,000 is the most he can borrow against the assets. In this situation, which is far from unusual, the seller may either accept the balance over a period of time or personally guarantee the difference to the new (or continuing) lending source. The seller's reasons for doing this can range from a generally positive feeling about the business potential and/or the prospective buyer to the more mundane reason of not having an alternative. If this is done, the seller will often agree to continue working (at a specified salary) until the balance is paid.

SUGGESTED READING

Gladstein, Arnold S. *The Complete Guide to Buying and Selling a Business.* New York: John Wiley & Sons, 1983.

8 The formal business structure: Legal and tax considerations

Two separate and distinct areas are involved in the determination of the appropriate business structure. The first concerns the technical and formal details of organization and the second, the organization and management of resources in a structure capable of performing the work of the enterprise. Because any technical organizational structure—individual or sole proprietorship, general or limited partnership, joint venture, or any of the various corporate forms—may be adapted to any operational structure, the choice of formal structure depends entirely on management's decision as to which structure best meets its nonoperational needs. (It is possible, for example, to have a board of directors in a sole proprietorship, depending on the inclination of the owner.)

The choice among these technical forms rests on judgments concerning tax factors and nontax factors. The nontax factors include:

1. Liability exposure.
2. Transferability of ownership.
3. Continuity.
4. Opportunities for initial and supplemental funding.
5. Cost of organization.

The tax factors include:

1. Treatment of income.
2. Possibilities of fringe benefits.
3. Possibilities of deferred payments.

The key to understanding the difference between the various formal structures is to view the sole proprietorship and the partnership as though they were simply an extension of the individuals involved while regarding the corporation as though it were a separate and independent entity created for the purpose of doing business. In effect, the business life of the individual proprietorship or partnership ceases with that of its owner or owners; the business life of the corporation is continuous.

A further and similar difference between the two exists in the handling of business profits and legal claims. For the individual involved in a sole proprietorship or a general partnership, there is no distinction between his business income and his personal income. His business profits are intermingled with his other sources of income, and they are taxed at the individual's appropriate rate. If there is a financial or legal claim against his business, it is as though the claim were against him personally, and he is liable for the satisfaction of that claim to the full extent of his resources (insurance considerations aside).

The corporate entity, on the other hand, is treated as though it were an independent body. It is taxed at a specially set rate (now 15 percent on the first $25,000, 18 percent on the second $25,000, 30 percent on the third $25,000, 40 percent on the fourth $25,000, and a maximum of 46 percent on the balance). The salaries of all its employees, whether shareholders or not, are taxed separately. Because it is owned by individuals outside the corporation, when its profits are distributed in the form of dividends, they are again taxed as regular income of the owners. Thus, for the owner/manager, the profits of a corporation are taxed twice, once as corporate profits and a second time as the income (dividends) of the individual shareholders. The corporation is liable for legal claims against it only to the amount of its assets.

A sole proprietorship, by definition, has only one owner, and his capital is the "equity" capital of the business. Should he decide to admit others to an equity position, he forms a partnership. If his partners actively participate and have an equal voice in the management of the business, they are considered general partners, and the partners' legal and financial liabilities (as in a sole proprietorship) include their partnership interest and their personal assets. If a partner supplies only capital and no services, exercising no control over the business affairs of the company (except for the right to inspect its books), he may join the company as a "limited" partner, participating like the other partners in its profits and losses, but with his liability limited to the amount he invests in the company. This form of partnership is often used in the so-called tax shelter situations.

Apart from the necessary licenses, no formalities are involved in starting a sole proprietorship, and consequently it is the least expensive business form to organize.

Partnerships have a similiar simplicity. Apart from certain tax regulations (and, in some states, the requirement that an initial informational certificate of partnership be filed), the state regulations that apply to partnerships are consistent with the essentially private nature of this business form, and their various provisions do not take effect unless the points in question have not been covered by an individualized private agreement. (Such private agreements deal with the percentage distribution of profits, authority, the buyout or sellout of interests, and other possible sources of disagreement.)

When a private agreement does not exist, or when points arise that it does not cover, in most states partnerships are covered by some variation of the Uniform Partnership Act. While the partnership acts differ from state to state, they typically provide arbitrary rules for the relationship between the partners. For example, one such rule in the New York Uniform Partnership Act states that profits are to be divided equally between partners regardless of capital contribution. This and other rules may be superseded by the specific partnership agreement of a particular enterprise. (It should be noted that stress-laden situations frequently arise in business partnerships, and the prudent businessman should provide a method of resolving even the most remote contingency in the partnership agreement.)

While there is no federal tax on partnerships, the IRS does require an informational partnership return. Certain states require partnership taxes.

A joint venture operates like a partnership except that it is formed to accomplish a specific task and is dissolved upon the completion of that task.

Corporations can range from very simple business structures with one shareholder to complex entities with many shareholders. Because the shareholders of a corporation, like limited partners, are not actively involved in running the business, they delegate their proportionate authority to a board of directors. The board of directors then delegates operating responsibility to selected officers. Control nevertheless rests with the shareholders, who can exercise it at any time. In situations where ownership interests are highly fragmented, united minority shareholders can have disproportionate influence.

Because the corporation, unlike the partnership, has a public identity, its operations are more directly supervised by the federal and state governments. These place a number of requirements on the corporation to protect the interests of the "absentee" owners. The requirements—mainly for the provision of information, annual meetings, minutes, and the like—are of a continuing nature. The jeopardy of "nuisance" suits, brought by individual shareholders for alleged "improper" activities by officers, is a constant threat to majority-selected corporate officers. Because the corporation acts as an individual, there are also rules concerning its conduct as a member of society. The specific rules for incorporation vary from state to state. Since the corporation is taxed separately, as an individual, it must comply with federal, state, and local tax requirements.

In addition to the advantages of separate existence, a principal advantage of the corporation is its ability to raise money through the sale of "equity" position (stock), "debts" (bonds), and variations in between. While both equity and debt financing are available to the sole proprietorship in different forms (equity as invested partnership capital, debt as loans), the paper issued by the corporation has the advantages of being transferable and of being subject to limitations as the amounts and the number of shareholders grow, and, as we have noted, the liability for the debt is technically restricted to the assets of the corporation. While limitations on voting rights can be imposed on various types of stock when issued, generally speaking, the greater the amount of the equity held by people other than the active managers, the less is the authority of those managers. Public scrutiny is a limitation of public presence.[1] Along the same lines, it should be realized that despite the limitations on personal liability provided by the corporate structure, personal financial guarantees for potential corporate liabilities are often sought by lending institutions to secure their interests.

The tax considerations of an individual proprietorship, a partnership, or a corporation, like the legal considerations, should be discussed with the appropriate professional counselors, but it is important here to note the differences in the handling of the salary, income, and various benefits of the principals and employees of individual proprietorships, partnerships, and corporations.

In all cases, the normal business expenses incurred by a working member of an enterprise (the costs necessary to carry out its functions) may be deducted before its profits are determined. However, when

[1]This distinction between corporations and the more private forms of business organization can be blurred by the regulations defining closely held corporations. Through such devices as limiting the number of shareholders and placing restrictions on the ability to sell or transfer stock, the government limits the public life of closely held corporations and consequently is less concerned with their compliance with the reporting and other requirements intended for public protection.

the owners of a corporation are working for it, they are considered employees of the corporation and therefore their salary is considered an expense of the corporation and deducted from corporate income before arriving at the corporate profit.

In a sole proprietorship or partnership, the salaries of the owners are regarded as synonymous with the profit after all other expenses are deducted from the income of the business entity and *is taxed as earned.* Depending on the income level of the entity, this may offset the advantage of being free from the double taxation of the corporate structure.

In the following illustration, assuming that the corporation, like the individual proprietorship, is owned by one individual, the actual tax owed would be the same for both (setting aside city and state provisions) because the $50,000 profit of the individual proprietorship would be taxed at the same rate as the $50,000 officer's salary of the corporation. When the figures change, this is no longer the case.

	Individual proprietorship	**Corporation**
Income	$400,000	$400,000
Costs and expenses	350,000	350,000
Officers' salaries	—	50,000
Profit	$ 50,000	—

In the next illustration, while the taxable income to the corporation's ownership is subject to how much of the $128,250 is actually distributed as dividends, the effective tax rate is clearly different in the two cases.

	Individual proprietorship	**Corporation**	
Income	$600,000	$600,000	
Costs and expenses	350,000	350,000	
Officers' salaries	—	50,000	
Profit	$250,000	200,000	
Business tax	—	71,750	
		$128,250	available for dividends

To provide for this difference, the Internal Revenue Service allows the corporation to elect to be taxed as a Subchapter S corporation, which in effect means that it can decide to have its tax computed as though it were an individual proprietorship or a partnership. This provision is confined to small corporations (those with no more than 35 shareholders) and is subject to limitations that prevent frequent change. For example, a corporation that decides it no longer wishes to be taxed under the Subchapter S regulation must wait five taxable years before it can again utilize that option. It can return to the corporate tax status immediately, but it must wait five years before again returning to Subchapter S status.[2]

The difficulty in making the choice between an individual proprietorship, a partnership, a corporation, and a Subchapter S corporation points up the clear need for the small businessman to seek professional assistance in technical areas outside his personal competence, particularly where substantial sums of money are involved. While the choice of a specific form of business entity seems to have relatively clear-cut aftertax implications for the owner-operator, that choice is complicated by the fact that corporate tax rates and individual tax rates are different at various levels of income (see Table 8–1). More important,

TABLE 8–1 Joint federal tax schedule

	Joint personal rates		Corporate rates
$7,600–11,900	15%		
$11,900–16,000	17	$0–25,000	15%
$24,600–29,900	26	$25,000–49,999	18
$29,900–35,200	30		
$35,200–45,800	35		
$45,800–60,000	40	$50,000–74,999	30
$60,000–85,600	44	$75,000–99,999	40
$85,600–109,400	48	Over $100,000	46
Over $109,400	50		

the question of fringe benefits is extremely complex. Decisions concerning such items as life insurance, disability insurance, medical insurance, direct medical reimbursement, interest-free loans, and the whole package of retirement benefits ranging from deferred income to pension possibilities involve a sophisticated understanding of current and pending tax law that is in most cases beyond the scope of the typical small businessman. The general principle concerning such benefits is that they must be granted to employees on a nondiscrimina-

[2]A corporation may also provide individual proprietorship benefits for its shareholders by adding the protection of Section 1244 of the tax code to its elections. According to Section 1244, if a corporation fails in its first two years of business, its shareholders can deduct the value of their stock from ordinary income on their personal returns.

tory basis, but where a corporation has a limited number of employees, considerable flexibility exists. The differences between the treatment of pension and deferred-income benefits that once existed between individual proprietorships and corporations have been considerably narrowed by the introduction of the Keogh plans and the IRAs.

As we pointed out at the beginning of this chapter, the choice of the technical structure of a company has little to do with the way it decides to organize in order to pursue its business purposes. (This subject will be discussed in the next chapter.) Whichever formal option the businessman selects, he should be aware that technical and legal control, the placement of authority, and continuity are prime considerations. A business association is not a grouping of friends or relatives. Individuals whose interests are identical at one point develop different interests. The ongoing business enterprise cannot afford to have its work and identity sacrificed to a clash of such interests. Whatever the informal relationships of the persons with equity in a business venture may be at the outset of activity or at various entry points, the relationships of those persons must be blended into a formal structure that anticipates possible conflicts in organizational life.

SUGGESTED READING

Zabalgovi, Judith Cowan. *How to Use Your Business or Profession as a Tax Shelter.* Reston, Va.: Reston Publishing, 1983.

9 The functioning of the individual and the group within the business enterprise

Effective human resource management is a significantly more important concern to the owner of the small business than to the manager of the larger business for three important reasons:

1. The small business lacks the depth and balance of resources—capital, equipment, and labor—characteristic of the larger firm, and therefore in the small business, the requirement that resources be maximized falls almost exclusively on the human component.
2. Since the small business lacks such advantages as size (see Chapter 3), its major resource in the development of an effective competitive strategy must lie in the area of "people skills"—creativity, drive, knowledge, understanding, awareness, and cooperation. The evocation of individual strengths and their mobilization into harmonious and reliable group strengths is a prime responsibility of the small businessman.
3. In the small business, the difficulties of personnel management are exacerbated by the fact, disclosed by the findings of social psychology, that the smaller the organizational structure, the more intense are the interpersonal relationships. Thus the need for understanding and dealing with such relationships becomes almost a special requirement of small business.

THE PYRAMID MODEL AND ITS LIMITATIONS

Traditional business theory suggests the use of a pyramid model to set forth the functional relationships of organizations. The design shown in Figure 9–1 is illustrative. "Staff" positions, appended horizontally, are considered advisory, while "line" positions, appended vertically, are designated as operational, with authority.

FIGURE 9–1 The pyramid model of business organization

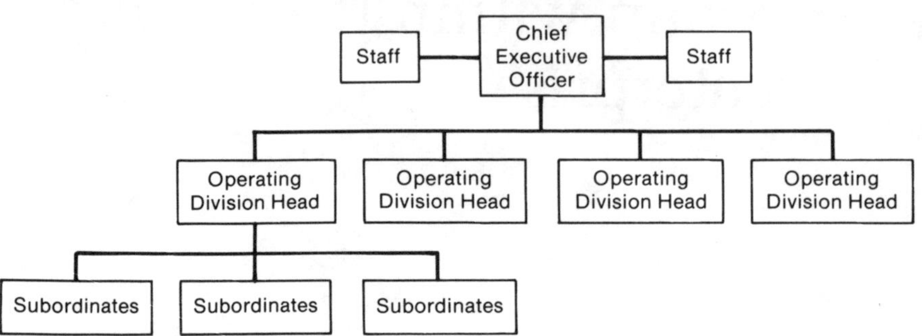

The value of the pyramid model as an operating mechanism depends on

1. A clearly defined chain of command.
2. Superior and outstanding knowledge at each supervisory level.
3. A division of work based on specialization.
4. A system of procedures and rules dealing with all business-related contingencies.
5. Human relationships characterized by dependence, submissiveness, and automatic responsiveness.

When this model is superimposed on the requirements and realities of today's small business, it becomes obvious immediately that the model doesn't work; the static, simple business situations that it was designed for no longer exist. As we have indicated throughout this book, the contemporary business environment is characterized by

1. Dynamic and unpredictable change, which calls for organizational sensitivity and flexibility.
2. Complex functional interrelationships, which call for an integration of specialized competences, a sharing and blending of information, a diffusion of knowledge.
3. A highly competitive market situation, which calls for a substantial degree of creativity.

Alongside these characteristics, and indeed making it possible to develop an organization capable of coping with them, we have a human resource with a newly developed sense of self-awareness. Authoritative research indicates that the modern worker, while seeking social interaction and the feeling of belongingness, responds to the demands of his own personality, his own individuality, through independently generated patterns of action. Thus, while today's worker has a different view of work than that recognized by the old pyramid model, while he would like to eliminate the distinction between the workplace and his external environment, he consciously or subconsciously realizes that this is possible only if the organization provides him with the vehicle he needs in order to satisfy his individual and highly complex basket of personal wants and needs. In this sense, he is no different from the consumer we discussed extensively earlier in this book. The workplace is the market to which the employee goes for need satisfaction. Effecting a harmonious marriage between the modern business task and today's human resource calls for a new concept of structure, one responsive both to the imperatives of business and to a newly refined definition of personal needs.

THE THEORETICAL UNDERPINNINGS OF HUMAN RESOURCE MANAGEMENT

Why and how some people perform better within an enterprise than do others, why some people continually strive for higher levels of achievement while others withdraw from the work of the enterprise, is an extremely complex question and one that is highly relevant to the problem of organizational structure. As we pointed out in Chapter 3, how creativity works is itself a difficult enough concept to deal with even if we do not attempt to meet the additional requirement of fostering its growth within the organization.

And yet unless the small businessman tries to harness individual drives to group tasks on an ongoing basis, and unless that effort is based on an intellectual and emotional grasp of modern personality theory, he will find that his enterprise will suffer chronically from inefficient and economically unsound resource utilization.

Consistent with our approach throughout this book, we will not offer a series of rules dealing with the human resource area; instead, we will outline the operative conceptual framework and invite the reader to develop an organizational form that serves his own ends.

Unfortunately, the necessary knowledge in the field of human resource management is located in a number of young disciplines—psychology, sociology, anthropology, and social psychology—all of which are outgrowths of the ancient study of philosophy. Dialogue in these disciplines tends to be obscure because of the highly technical vocabulary preferred by the knowledgeable academicians. Moreover, these disciplines lack the universally accepted findings characteristic of other sciences. Their theoretical basis is usually empirical, clinically grounded in observations of selected laboratory groups or of individuals in psychotherapy. Further, as we will indicate, the complexities involved in the study of personality make it extremely difficult to apply general hypotheses to specific individuals in specific situations, particularly if in-depth profiles of these individuals are unavailable.

Despite these troublesome reservations and despite our continuing effort to avoid abstractions, we feel that an understanding of the basic tenets of the disciplines in question is absolutely essential for the manager of a small business. The great interest in human resource management and the absence of any clear-cut, easily interpreted set of reliable guidelines has spawned a plethora of "pop" books, articles, and movies that offer a variety of simplistic approaches. Without a basic understanding of the existent theory, it is impossible to eliminate the simplistic approaches or to construct a workable approach to the problem of organization.

The development of such an understanding is facilitated for the nonprofessional student of personality by the fact that specific distinctions concerning the "when" and "how" of various influences are less important to him than the realization that these influences are operative, that they exist in the particular context in which the business structure must function. Thus, while certain generalizations may overstate one theory and understate another, for practical purposes the conclusions may still be valid.

PERSONALITY THEORY AND ITS ORGANIZATIONAL IMPLICATIONS

Modern personality theory tells us that the human being is born with certain instincts and needs. One set of these needs is referred to as cognitive. It includes the need for knowledge and understanding. From birth on, the individual strives to satisfy these needs through growth.

Another set of needs, mentioned previously, was articulated by the late Abraham Maslow. This set is presented as a hierarchy of five types of needs:

1. The physiological needs—the needs for food, rest, and so on. Meeting these needs complements the joint automatic effort of the body and mind to maintain a constant, normal, healthy state.
2. The safety needs, which include security, stability, dependence,

freedom from fear, and freedom from anxiety and chaos. Structure, order, law, and limits help to satisfy these needs.

3. The needs for love, belongingness, and affectionate relationships—for a place in a group. Fears of loneliness, ostracism, rejection, friendlessness, and rootlessness, are manifestations of the basic need for contact and intimacy.
4. The needs for self-respect, self-esteem, and the esteem of others. These needs first appear in the desire for strength, achievement, adequacy, mastery, and confidence. Later they appear in the desire for reputation, prestige, status, glory, dominance, recognition, attention, importance, dignity, appreciation, and so forth.
5. The need for self-actualization—the need for the individual to become actually what he perceives himself to be potentially.

Maslow conceived these needs to be, in substantial degree, sequential: the gratification of one type of need leads to the emergence of the next type. An unsatisfied need becomes a principal preoccupation (to the exclusion of other needs) until it is satiated. According to Maslow, the highest level of need, the need for self-actualization, is never fully satisfied and therefore provides an unending challenge to the individual who reaches that level.

In attempting to relate Maslow to the concept of organization and using his perception of needs as background, we approach the field of social psychology and begin to deal with the subject of the developing "self," the "person" who emerges as the product of the interaction between the individual and his environment, the person who comes to the group. This interaction generally takes place in three forms:

1. The imagination of our appearance to other persons—family, playmates, co-workers.
2. The imagination of others' judgment of our appearance—approval/disapproval, admiration/contempt, like/dislike, and so on.
3. Our reaction to these perceptions—pride, confidence, shame, and so on.

Thus, through the blending of many and varied social experiences, the individual personality comes into existence. The developmental process begins at birth and continues throughout life. Because the life of each individual is a unique mix of the social interaction that he has undergone, no two individuals are exactly alike, and because the individual's experience and social interaction are continuous, no single individual is the same at two different points in his life. It also follows, as we will point out shortly, that even at a given point in time, no individual has the same relationship to different individuals or situations.

The degree to which a particular experience or social interaction influences personality corresponds to the quality of the individual's participation in it—to what some psychologists speak of as the general richness of the "behavior setting." The depth of this influence depends on the time spent in the setting, the individual's role in the setting (participant, observer, etc.), and the intensity of the experience—how close the individual is to the center of the situation. Thus, for example, the family experience during childhood tends to play a dominant role in personality development because the individual's participation in that experience is usually quite intense. With reference to Maslow's need hierarchy, it is easy to see how different types of childhood experience shape later feelings about such needs as those for belonging, confidence, and affection. Team sports, school activities, and religious training are other behavior settings that may shape a particular personality.

In order to understand the problems caused by the intermingling of distinct and constantly varying personalities within the organization, a note on the varying ways in which they express themselves is necessary.

The messages that are delivered and received in the process of social interaction, the information and the experience that is exchanged, are communicated by means of "symbols." These symbols are the language through which a particular group "speaks." The term *symbol* refers to anything from the spoken word to clothes to body signals. The meaning of specific symbols varies in different behavior settings. Kissing, a common means of symbolic interaction, for example, may indicate the resolution of an argument, a reward, a simple acknowledgment of presence, or extreme tenderness, depending on the user and his "language" background. Different symbols have different meanings to different people. Dress is an obvious illustration. An outfit worn with one expressive intention by a member of a particular social group may be totally misunderstood by a member of another group.

Similarly, "norms" are distinctive to settings. Norms are the traditional values of social aggregates. As an individual comes into contact with a specific setting, he learns to interpret its values, its norms, and to the degree that the experience permits, he adapts those norms to his own value system.

Norms, like symbols, vary with different social aggregates: Killing is desirable in an army and permissible within certain criminal cultures, but it is generally unacceptable behavior in normal business activity. Honesty is not always regarded as desirable, and stealing is not always regarded as undesirable. In some societies, competitiveness is welcome; in others, it is frowned upon.

The individual's acquisition and internalization of a particular set of norms develop his sense of "ought." He learns what is expected of him in a particular social situation; he formulates a personal program through which he must run his needs; he identifies the norms—the "oughts"—and learns what kind of behavior will enable him to achieve his objectives. The manager cannot deal with the need for satisfaction within the organization or understand such abstractions as esteem or affection unless he is able to interpret the norms involved in their definition in terms of specific individuals. Otherwise, even if he recognizes the symbols through which esteem, affection, and so on are indicated, how can he interpret the individually derived norms, the oughts, that produce them? What may seem to be an indication of esteem in one case may seem to be an indication of disapproval in another. In terms of the "ought" of killing, an act that generates rewards in one situation generates punishments in another.

While the killing illustration is rather extreme, it is essential to remember that the value systems of different individuals have been produced by varied and unique combinations of social interaction. The differences in the nature and intensity of their experiences with national culture, religion, work, family, athletics, and so forth will make different behavior normative to different individuals. Indeed, the individual must be greater than the sum of his parts because participation in different behavior settings requires him to be able to utilize different aspects of normative behavior in different situations. The individual assumes different social roles in anticipation of different expectations, different values: the father of four may be an authority figure in one aspect of his existence and a subordinate in another; a professional athlete may be expected to offer tenderness and intimacy in one role and hostility in another. Thus, as we noted earlier, the same individual may appear in two completely different lights at a particular time. It is appropriate to note here that *persona* is the Latin word for mask.

The overwhelming but undeniable fact of organizational life is that it is peopled by highly individualized selves, these ever-changing products of complex backgrounds who bring their sets of needs to the group for satisfaction (see Figure 9–2).

As the task of the businessman in understanding his organizational structure starts to take shape, it is important for him to pause and reflect upon his own complexity as well as that of his fellow worker. It is important for him to feel the baggage that both he and his fellow workers carry. It is essential that he realize that the person to whom he is talking is a person who comes from a different place, along a different path. Regardless of how similar the businessman's needs may be to

FIGURE 9–2 Individual needs and the group

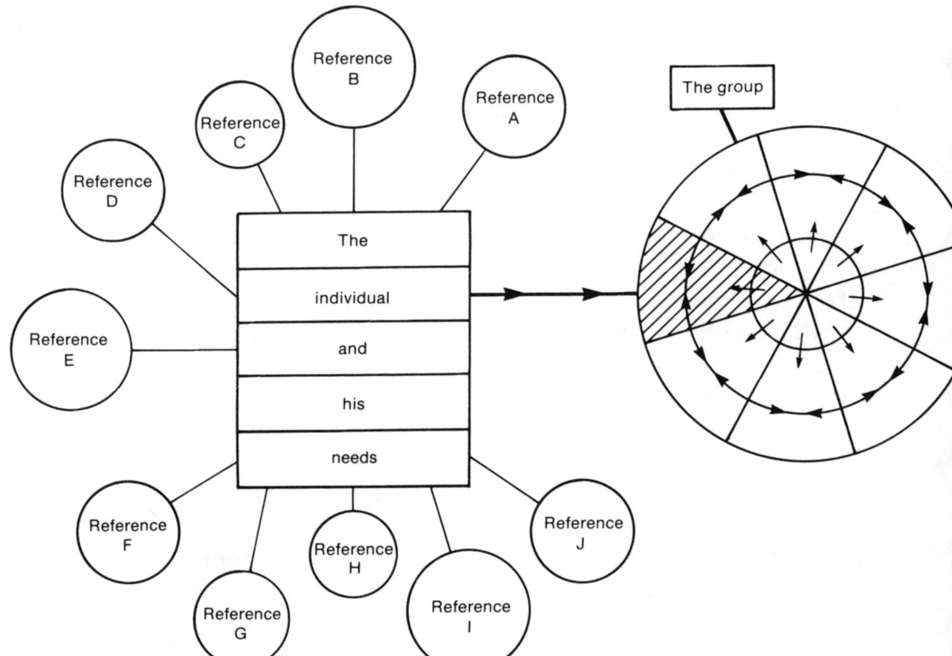

those of his fellow workers, the ways in which those needs are seen and the forms in which they must be realized may be more different than even the most perceptive businessman might expect.

PSYCHOLOGICAL ASPECTS OF HUMAN RESOURCE MANAGEMENT

The owner of a small business must remember at all times that any one of the anxiety-producing elements—the striving toward self-fulfillment, the identity confusion caused by role conflict, the need to select symbols and norms that may be appropriate to one situation and not to another—can lead the most conscientious worker to utilize smaller and smaller proportions of his potential through withdrawal from the social aggregate (alienation) or through failure to live with its value system (anomie).

The problems of managing human resources, whether the group involved consists of 2, 20, or 200 people, must be viewed in this context. For the organizational structure to work, the idea that determines the shape and nature of authority and responsibility and enables the organization to accomplish its goals must have as its basis an understanding of the factors that encourage people to work together while attempting to realize their individual potential. Unless the work environment is built upon this foundation, an effective organizational structure cannot be developed.

A particularly helpful way of looking at the subject has been devised by Harry Levinson in his book *The Executive.* Dealing primarily with the individual in the group, Levinson separates the human resource task into two functions, responses to what he calls the "ministration" and "maturation" needs.

Satisfying ministration needs

According to Levinson, the organization satisfies its "ministration" needs by addressing itself to the Maslow hierarchy of needs. Depending on its perception of the need level attained by its employees, it may emphasize security, protection, stability, dependence, freedom from fear, the need for belongingness, support, inclusion, achievement, adequacy, mastery, self-respect, self-esteem, esteem from others, and so forth. These needs exist in varying degrees throughout the organization; therefore, the basic ministration task is to create an environment in which they can be satisfied.

Because, as Maslow pointed out, the various types of needs are sequential, the initial approach must be to determine the individual requirements of the persons involved—for whom is security most important, for whom is mastery most important, and so forth. A helpful tool for this purpose is a written profile of each of the organization members. This device forces the manager to think the problem through.

As the manager attempts to create a work situation capable of satisfying these needs, he must remember that central to the success of the ministration effort is the recognition of the complexity of the norms, symbols, and the other accoutrements of the changing, developing self. The organization cannot afford to be overwhelmed by the diversity of its personnel; rather, it must utilize that diversity as a source of strength. The eccentricities of the organization and its members—the ideas, values, and oughts peculiar to specific groups and persons—must be faced honestly and openly. They must be explained to new members.

The symbols that represent rewards and recognition vary with each person. A pat on the back may give one person a wonderfully positive feeling but make another person think, "They don't understand me at all." Shorter or different working hours are an easily misunderstood form of compensation. Titles are subject to a variety of interpretations. *Appropriate* is a word that assumes great importance in human resource management. The idea of appropriateness is consistent with the relatively new "cafeteria benefits" approach, in which a company makes compensation available in a variety of forms and the individual chooses among them.

Responding to the ministration needs takes many forms. The initial and ongoing relationships must overcome a natural fear of failing that might keep a person from trying. There must be a recognition of interpersonal anxiety that openly deals with the idiosyncrasies of co-workers and the barriers to action. Answers to such difficulties must be encouraged. There must be guidelines as to how to get along psychologically as well as physically.

Particularly relevant guidelines for meeting the ministration requirement of the small business that relies on upwardly mobile persons who are relatively free from Maslow's lower-level anxieties may be found in three well-researched works. These works relate behaviorist theory to the upper levels of the need structure. (The basic assumption of behaviorism is that behavior is a function of consequences; people are more likely to repeat an action if its consequences are pleasant.)

The authors of two of these works, V. H. Vroom and Abraham Korman, have similar viewpoints. In *Work and Motivation*, Vroom developed the (E)xpectation Theory, which postulated that (E)xpectation leads to (P)erformance and (P) leads to (O)utcome. The performer expects something to happen as a result of a particular performance. When he feels that the completion of performance brings satisfactory results, his expectation rises, and consequently he moves to the next higher level of performance.

In *Industrial and Organizational Psychology*, Korman reinterprets this approach in his own theory of "self-implementation." The higher a worker's perception of personal competence is, the more effective will be the performance. Environments conducive to self-confidence increase the likelihood of getting competent performance.

Korman goes on to state the following:

1. Persons who are told that they are incompetent to achieve a specific task, even though they have had no previous experience with that task, will perform worse than persons who are told that they are competent to achieve the task.
2. Self-perceived ability based on previous performance is positively related to later performance.
3. The more a person has failed in the past, the less he or she will aspire to in the future.
4. Groups that have failed previously set their goals in ways that increase the probability of their failing again.

5. Persons and groups of low self-esteem are less likely to achieve difficult goals that they have set for themselves than are persons and groups of high self-esteem.

Bernard Rosenbaum's *How to Motivate Today's Workers* takes this theory a step further (and makes it particularly applicable to the individuals who fill today's managerial ranks) by focusing directly on Maslow's esteem need. He relates this need directly to the work environment, further clarifying the concept of ministration. When the individual's need is for esteem, Rosenbaum points out, the organization cannot sit by and wait for him to fail, for his self-esteem to be eroded. It must work to foster success by

1. Setting goals that are understood, believable, and acceptable to the individual and specifically defining objectives in terms of such things as how much and when. (A directive to work harder or faster or more efficiently does not foster success because unless the desired performance can be measured *in some way*, it cannot be used as a device for personal satisfaction.)
2. Providing the training necessary to succeed.
3. Recognizing the achievement of the desired performance when it occurs.[1]

It is not possible to list all of the actions that will enable the individual to meet his various needs within the organizational structure. What is essential is an understanding that the individual reacts positively to the gratification of his needs and negatively to failures to gratify them; ministration to those needs is therefore crucial to the health of the organization. The need for belongingness, for acceptance, inclines the individual toward the organization. As his needs are met within the organization, they escalate. As he perceives favorable outcomes following his performance, he seeks higher levels of personal achievement while at the same time developing an attachment to the organization that provides the key to the satisfaction of his needs.

Satisfying maturation needs

Maturation needs differ from ministration needs in that they are concerned primarily with the quality of performance rather than its encouragement. As we have pointed out earlier in this chapter and

[1]Frederick Herzberg has analyzed two types of job factors, "satisfiers" and "dissatisfiers." Dissatisfiers, such things as salary and good working conditions, are significant only in their absence. Satisfiers provide gratification in Maslow's sense—achievement, recognition, responsibility, advancement, and pleasure in the work itself.

more fully in the chapter devoted to strategy, success for a small business most often lies in the area of creativity. And yet it is often felt that creativity is incompatible with the structure necessary to a functioning business entity because it involves nonlinear thinking, departures from the normal routines. When Alexander the Great offered help to Diogenes, Diogenes is said to have replied, "Stand out of my light." While there are those who feel that limited control should be the manager's posture in relation to his creative people, this approach usually encounters great difficulty.

If we dwell for a minute on our earlier discussion of expectation theory and the pertinent elements of the hierarchy of needs, it becomes obvious that the organization has much to offer the creative person in terms of support, rewards, esteem, and so forth. The task of the manager is to encourage this person's efforts while harnessing them to the larger group, whose energy, pride, and stature are enhanced by those efforts.

The current "hot phrase" for the idea that works in this connection is "corporate culture." In the terms that we have already discussed extensively in this chapter, this comprises the norms, values, and oughts that identify acceptable behavior in a particular corporate environment. While the environment that a small business needs in order to function effectively must encourage freedom and creativity, the general values of our society and the functional requirements of an organization make it difficult to establish such an environment. Even in those cases where management believes that a system encouraging individual initiative and creativity is desirable, two formidable obstacles produced by earlier conditioning must be overcome:

1. A general hostility within our society to nonconformity. That hostility is backed by a lifetime spent in seeking the "right answer" through sequential thinking (as discussed in Chapter 3).
2. A common belief that "power" is a symbol of responsibility and authority.

Because these cultural values are ingrained in our society, positive steps are necessary to inculcate different cultural values.

The first and most crucial step in establishing a corporate culture that encourages initiative and creativity is the development of an understanding on the part of all employees that without initiative and creativity, the business cannot succeed or survive.

It follows that there must be clearly understood rewards for behavior that meets the standards of the desired corporate culture. If, for example, creative thinking is to be encouraged, then *all* new ideas must be rewarded in some way. If initiative is to be encouraged, then *every* instance of initiative must be acknowledged and supported. This does not mean that the company must adopt every new idea that an employee advances. But it does mean that the initiator of a rejected idea must be given a full, believable explanation of its rejection and a supportive reaction to his effort.

The idea of initiative runs directly counter to the concept of "power." The words commonly associated with power—*territory, coercion, sovereignty*—are words that do not permit subordinates and associates to undertake the kind of decision making that leads to personal growth or the type of independent action that builds self-confidence. The manager must substitute the concepts of collaboration and reason for the concept of power, again through action that reinforces the corporate culture. (If through supportive action the supervisor learns that the development of subordinates is a value of the company, then he will recognize that his path to self-fulfillment is not power but the success of subordinates.)

CONCLUSIONS

The choice of an organizational structure must take into consideration the various points raised in this chapter. It is not the lines running from box to box that make an organization work; it is not the functional definition of responsibility that provides momentum. Perhaps, in recognition of the interrelationships of group members and supervisors, a configuration such as this one

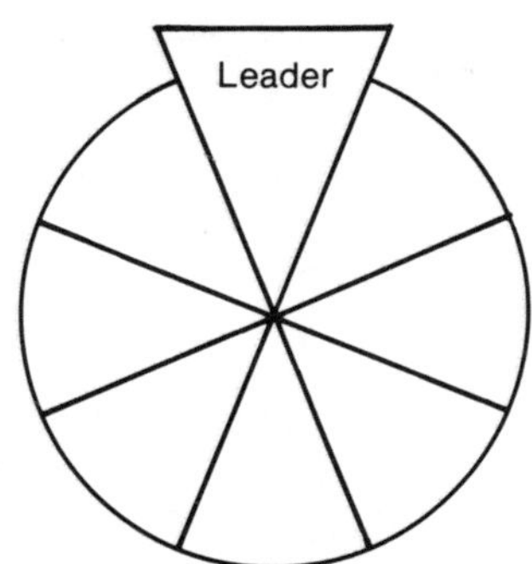

should be substituted for the traditional grouping:

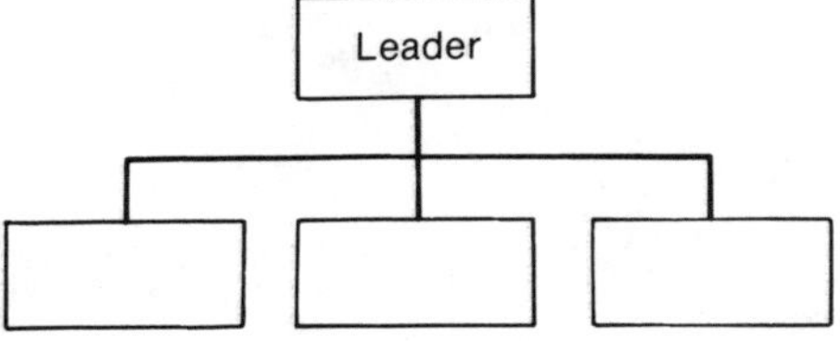

The advantages of traditional forms of organization are obvious; clear lines of communication are necessary; and accountability is essential. But in a small business there is also a need to have each member of the group feel a sense of responsibility both for his own performance and for the destiny of the enterprise. The structural terms of the organization must make that possible.

SUGGESTED READINGS

Anastasi, Anne. *Fields of Applied Psychology.* 2d ed. New York: McGraw-Hill, 1979.

Bales, Robert Freed. *Personality and Interpersonal Behavior.* New York: Holt, Rinehart & Winston, 1970.

Bennis, Warren G. *Organization Development.* Reading, Mass.: Addison-Wesley Publishing, 1969.

Korman, Abraham. *Industrial and Organizational Psychology.* Englewood Cliffs, N.J.: Prentice-Hall, 1971.

Levinson, Harry. *The Executive.* Cambridge, Mass.: Harvard University Press, 1981.

Nisbet, Robert. *The Social Bond.* New York: Alfred A. Knopf, 1970.

Rosenbaum, Bernard L. *How to Motivate Today's Workers.* New York: McGraw-Hill, 1982.

Vroom, V. H. *Work and Motivation.* New York: John Wiley & Sons, 1964.

10 Final steps (including the business plan)

Should you decide to pursue the task of owning and operating a small business further, there are certain matters that you should deal with early in the process.

1. If you lack experience in the field you selected, it is highly desirable that you gain some practical background in a similar field. It's worth the time. The various lending institutions feel that the experience of the prospective borrower is extremely important in evaluating risk, and this belief is based on valid historical data.
2. If you are planning to open a business, you should seek professional help, both by consulting a CPA and by communicating with professionals in the field. This approach should be supplemented by reading and by discussions with the SCORE and ACT people of the SBA.
3. If you admit others to an equity position in your business in the expectation that they will help you in its operation, you should seek compatibility as well as complementary strengths. Interpersonal difficulties grow geometrically rather than arithmetically. The addition of a third ownership interest alters the interactions between the first two. Thus the determination of how many equity members should be admitted is a serious business decision with many ramifications.
4. Whether or not you plan to approach a public or private funding source, you should prepare a business plan.

Because some readers will no doubt use this chapter as a guide to the preparation of such a plan, we will add specific suggestions to our usual more generalized, conceptual approach to the subject.

A "business plan" is a detailed, formal statement of what a business is and will be, together with the supporting statistical data. It is, in fact, the sum total of this book applied to a specific situation. Consequently, our discussion of the preparation of such a plan provides an excellent opportunity for review.

The business plan is used for three major purposes:

1. To set forth the objectives of a business in a way that permits management to measure progress toward their achievement.
2. To provide a vehicle for the communication of goals and strategies.
3. As the business "prospectus" for funding resources.

Depending on the use that is being made of a business plan, the emphasis on its various purposes will vary. Regardless of the use, however, the formal effort to develop such a plan encourages a detached view of the owners' aims. That alone would justify the effort. As we have pointed out throughout this book, while intelligence, common sense, creativity, and drive are important to the success of a business venture, planning is indispensable. While a business plan is not always a requirement in the solicitation of financial support, it is evidence of the ability of management to view its task realistically and as such can be a significant aid in any and all projects.

The three major sections of a business plan are: (1) the description of the business, (2) the financial data, and (3) documentary information supporting the major hypotheses.

THE DESCRIPTION OF THE BUSINESS (SECTION 1 OF THE BUSINESS PLAN)

The description of the business deals with the material covered in Chapters 2, 3, and 4 of this book. It begins with a simple statement of the target customer's needs and how the business intends to satisfy those needs. If the business plan is to be used as a financing proposal, it should also include responses to the following questions:

1. Who is asking for the money?
2. What is the formal structure of the business (partnership, corporation, etc.)?
3. How much money is needed?
4. What is the money needed for, and how will it be used?

5. How will the money be either repaid (in the case of a loan) or integrated into the capital structure (in the case of equity financing)?

The objective of the business description is to explain what the business is, how you are going to run it, and why you think it will be successful. Thus the follow-up to this description must include:

1. Your evaluation of the market.
2. Your perception of the competitive environment.
3. Your response to the situation as you see it.

Supporting documents such as market research should be noted here and appear in detailed form in Section 3. This separation of Section 1 narrative from Section 3 detail is important so that ideas and information flow in a clear and simple manner. The writer must avoid the tendency to overwhelm the reader.

The thoroughness and detail with which these statements and the supporting documents are attacked will be a major contribution to the credibility of the business plan. Depending on whether it's an existing business, a new business, or a buyout, you will want to indicate the level of your experience and that of your associates, your degree of commitment, your study of similar businesses, your investigation of the trade suppliers, sales and price trends, and your major customers.

Guidelines for Section 1 of the business plan

A. The overview.
   1. The financial proposal, with a summary of the financial background.
   2. The purpose of the business in terms of the consumer needs that it will satisfy.
   3. The qualifications of the management.
   4. The formal structure (sole proprietorship, etc.) and the current status (new business, expansion, takeover, etc.) of the business.
   5. Outside professionals who have been involved (CPA, lawyer, designer, etc.).

B. Why the business will be successful.
   1. Evaluation of the competitive environment, including a summary of all the relevant information concerning the strength of competition, suppliers, and general market trends.
   2. The strategic approach, including a summary of the marketing research, the marketing program, and, when significant, the qualifications of nonmanagement personnal.*

*The competitive environment, marketing research, marketing program, and significant qualifications of nonmanagement personnel are detailed in Section 3 of the business plan.

This section must demonstrate not only that you have a good product or service but that the product or service is related to a viable target market of which you are knowledgeable and to which you have a realistic approach.

THE FINANCIAL DATA (SECTION 2 OF THE BUSINESS PLAN)

The financial documents necessary for Section 2 of the business plan are discussed in detail in Chapter 5 of this book. They should include:

1. Profit and loss statements, actual (if available) and pro forma, for at least three years (depending on when financial stability and loan repayment is accomplished).
2. Ratio analysis for industry comparison if possible.
3. The start-up plan.
4. A break-even analysis in graph form, with S curve projection in support.
5. A cash flow statement for the period corresponding to item 1 above, monthly for at least one year, quarterly thereafter.
6. Balance sheets, actual (if available) and pro forma, for appropriate years.
7. A detailed schedule of anticipated sales where possible—percentage of available rooms occupied, number of meals served, original and repeat customers, transactions, and so on.
8. A detailed schedule of fixed and leased assets—new and used—with their cost or an estimate of their market value and an indication of their state of repair with respect to their prospective use.

Particularly when the business plan is for internal use, a method of comparing actual performance with planned performance and a specific time schedule for review are indispensable. The comparison of actual performance with planned performance is known as deviation or variance analysis; it corresponds to the planning budget in Chapter 5. This project can be as simple or as complex as management decides to make it, but it should include sales, gross margin, and profitability, and it should note deviations in any of the significant variables.

SUPPORTING DOCUMENTS (SECTION 3 OF THE BUSINESS PLAN)

The items included in the supporting documents (Section 3) will vary with the individual business. Pertinent items may include personnel résumés, books, newspaper or magazine articles, cost quotations for marketing projects or prospective asset purchases, personal income statements, letters of reference, letters of intent, or orders on hand. Too much detail is not possible.

In discussing the competitive environment, it is desirable when possible to mention such specifics as how big the apparent market is; who has what share; what the "health" of the competition is; who has succeeded in this field, who has failed, and why; what share you are planning on; and why you believe your estimates are realistic. You should deal with prospective as well as current competition and with the requirements for market entry, including regulations, technology, and experience where applicable.

A point-by-point comparison of your product or service with the products or services of your competitors is appropriate. Assume no information on the part of your reader. Where this aspect of the plan is for external use, do not hesitate to include a physical demonstration of your product or service. Where test marketing or expert opinion has been utilized, include details on the results as well as details on the results of any other marketing research that has been undertaken. If location is important, discuss traffic counts and patterns, parking, and so forth.

Information on established relationships with suppliers—particularly information on credit terms, reliability of supply, and the availability of "unique" support—can be an important part of this section.

The marketing program should be explained fully. If advertising and other sales promotion prototypes have been developed, they should be included.

Depending on the size of the enterprise, information concerning individual employees or the employees as a whole can be included, together with salary schedules.

SUGGESTED READINGS

Bangs, David H., Jr., and William R. Osgood. *Business Planning Guide.* Portsmouth, N.H.: Upstart Publishing, 1981.

Citibank Banking Guide for Growing Businesses. New York: Citibank, 1981.

Index

C

D

E

F

T

U

V

W–Z